W0232604

INDIA
on the
MOVE

ADVANCE PRAISE FOR THE BOOK

'I have known Marya Shakil for many years and seen the way she has grown into a skilled political reporter, anchor and analyst. She has covered the ground-level shifts taking place in the country today and tracked the high-level machinations in the corridors of power. It has led her to capture the two competing narratives dominating the country today, with her co-author, Narendra Nath, in her book, *India on the Move: When Jai Shri Ram Met Bharat Mata ki Jai*. The book focuses on the major social and political developments in the last ten years, which have sharply polarized the national discourse'—**Neerja Chowdhury, author of *How Prime Ministers Decide***

'The book *India on the Move: When Jai Shree Ram Met Bharat Mata ki Jai* presents an interesting account of events which shaped the 2024 Lok Sabha elections. Various accounts presented in the book not only help in connecting various dots, but make one feel as if one personally witnessed those events or was part of those conversations. An account of various interesting discussions, connecting various dots, has been presented in the book. A must-read for all those interested in the 2024 Lok Sabha elections verdict in particular and the Indian elections and politics in general'—**Sanjay Kumar, professor, Centre for the Study of Developing Societies**

'*India on the Move: When Jai Shri Ram Met Bharat Mata ki Jai* offers a compelling time-travel journey through a decade of pivotal events that have shaped India's political and social landscapes. The authors deliver a meticulous and unbiased account, allowing readers to draw their own conclusions about the impact and significance of these moments. This book stands out for its innovative approach and thorough analysis, providing a thought-provoking perspective on contemporary Indian politics. A must-read for anyone interested in understanding the forces that have shaped last few years India'—**Javed Akhtar, poet and lyricist**

'Narendra Nath has written a valuable analysis of the reasons why the BJP performed well below its expectations in the 2024 elections, and why the INDIA bloc performed far above its expectations. It provides reassurance that India is not sold on the Hindutva message. Jobs, inflation and other daily problems matter far more to the Indian electorate than the inauguration of a Ram temple. Indians are intensely religious, but a Ram temple will not produce millions of jobs or tame prices. The Modi brand is powerful, no doubt, but can no longer ensure electoral victory on its own. The BJP has been bruised and the Congress has been infused with new hope. We are back to the great uncertainties of a democracy'—**Swaminathan Aiyar, Indian economist and journalist**

INDIA

on the
MOVE

when
JAI SHRI RAM
met
BHARAT MATA KI JAI

MARYA SHAKIL

NARENDRA NATH MISHRA

EBURY
PRESS

An imprint of Penguin Random House

EBURY PRESS

Ebury Press is an imprint of the Penguin Random House group of companies whose addresses can be found at global.penguinrandomhouse.com

Published by Penguin Random House India Pvt. Ltd
4th Floor, Capital Tower 1, MG Road,
Gurugram 122 002, Haryana, India

First published in Ebury Press by Penguin Random House India 2024

ISBN 9780143467311

Typeset in Adobe Caslon Pro by MAP Systems, Bengaluru, India
Printed at Thomson Press India Ltd, New Delhi

www.penguin.co.in

Contents

Prologue

The mandate of 4 June 2024 marked not just an electoral outcome but a pivotal moment in the ongoing saga of India's democratic journey. To say that it brought about one of the most intriguing twists in the Indian political scenario, will be stating the obvious. Up until the day of the results, not only was BJP's victory being considered imminent, but its magnitude also seemed significant. Poll results, however, delivered a surprise. In a rather unexpected development, BJP's tally stood at 240, well below not just its dream figure of 400 but also the majority mark of 272. While the Bharatiya Janata Party (BJP)-led National Democratic Alliance (NDA) was able to form the government, it was with an unnervingly narrow margin. The Opposition, on the other hand—which had been written off by exit polls and poll pundits alike—put on a far stronger show than expected, bagging 232 of the 543 parliamentary seats.

Prime Minister Narendra Modi had earlier asserted that he went to people with hope in 2014, trust in 2019 and guarantee in 2024. While the 2024 verdict didn't quite live up to expectations, the fact was that during the 2014–24 decade, the BJP steadily strengthened its hold on the political landscape. In 2014, the BJP won 282 seats on its own, while the NDA's tally stood at 336. They only went on to better the tally in 2019 when the BJP alone won 303 seats and its allies added another fifty. Poll numbers apart, the 2014–24 period, with Narendra

Modi at its helm, was marked by several decisions that had a profound impact on India's political, economic and social landscapes. Demonetization, implementation of Goods and Services Tax (GST), revocation of Article 370, implementation of the Citizenship Amendment Act (CAA) and 2019 surgical strikes were only some decisions that the BJP was able to weave into its political narrative convincingly. Additionally, this period also saw the rise of nationalism and an increased focus on Hindu identity. The slogan '*Jai Shri Ram* (Hail Lord Ram)', with its historical and religious connotations, was increasingly used as a political tool to consolidate the Hindu vote bank. Similarly, '*Bharat Mata ki Jai*' emerged as a chant that combined patriotism with religious undertones.

The fulfilment of the promise of the Ram temple at Ayodhya, a couple of months ahead of the elections, seemed to be a final clincher and an important agenda of the BJP's electoral campaign. The foundation stone for the Ram temple particularly became a symbolic milestone, heralding not just a culmination of the BJP's long-standing ideological goals, but also its political aspirations. Ahead of the consecration ceremony, advertisements and roadside hoardings showed the prime minister holding the hand of a five-year-old child symbolizing Ram Lalla—thus demonstrating the BJP's slogan '*Ye laye hain Ram ko*', he has brought Ram to us, and implying that the people of the country should vote for the people who had given Lord Ram his rightful place. On the appointed date, the prime minister himself, on behalf of the state, carried out the consecration of the Ram Temple in Ayodhya. It was believed that the temple would usher in a new era of Hindu nationalist pride in the country and ensure a third term for the party. Sure enough, opinion polls and narratives began hinting that under Narendra Modi's leadership, the BJP was set for a hat-trick victory.

While the BJP rose from strength to strength, the Opposition, on the other hand, had struggled to find a cohesive narrative. Bihar Chief Minister Nitish Kumar's attempt to unify the Opposition through the Indian National Developmental Inclusive Alliance (INDIA) bloc in 2023—a multiparty alliance—had initially seemed promising. However, by 2024, the alliance had begun to unravel. Nitish Kumar himself had left the Opposition's fold and returned, for the umpteenth time, to the NDA. It was also widely believed that the Opposition lacked any solid narrative against BJP's slogans of '*Jai Shri Ram*' and '*Bharat Mata ki Jai*', which had by now become rallying cries. As the elections approached, opposition leaders also had a hard time presenting a united front against the BJP's formidable electoral machine. There was lack of consensus on seat-sharing for the longest time, and the very public fights between Aam Aadmi Party (AAP) and Congress or Congress and Trinamool Congress (TMC) did not invite confidence. To make matters worse, several opposition leaders, including Delhi Chief Minister Arvind Kejriwal and former Jharkhand Chief Minister Hemant Soren found themselves behind bars just before polls, while several others were under central agencies' scanners. It did not look like a level playing field by any stretch of the imagination.

Buoyed by these happenings, the BJP was confident of its victory. '*Abki baar 400 paar*', Modi had declared right from the early stage of his campaign, sure that BJP will secure its aspiration of gaining 400 seats. In our interview with PM Modi during his Patna roadshow, he was emphatic in saying, '*Pure desh mein Bhartiya Janta party aur NDA ko 400 paar karane ka dhridh sankalp hai . . . Zabardast aandhi Uttar dakshin purab paschim sab taraf hai.*' The entire nation has made this strong resolution to ensure that BJP and NDA cross the 400 mark. There seems to be a strong wind in its favour.

The exit polls after the final phase of voting also went on to predict an overwhelming majority for the BJP. Over a dozen exit polls conducted by various agencies and media organizations, predicted that NDA will secure anywhere between 316 and 400 seats—not quite the 400 paar the BJP had envisioned but close enough. Banking on the exit poll predictions of continuity and political stability, the share markets recorded a massive jump. Both Sensex and Nifty, the indices of the Bombay Stock Exchange and the National Stock Exchange, hit record highs following the exit polls.[1]

Then came the decisive day of the election results. The BJP's roaring slogan of '*Abki baar 400 paar*' started dying down as the figures began trickling in. Early trends showed that the BJP could scrape through but with a shrivelled majority. The results revealed that the BJP had managed to secure 240 seats. While analysts described it as a split verdict, one thing was clear—it wasn't a verdict that was swayed by mega narratives and hyperboles. Many also saw it as a win for democracy.

Does the verdict mean that the era of nationalistic politics, which peaked for a decade from 2014, is now in decline? At the very least, is there a pause in its trajectory? It will be worthwhile looking at some of the aspects that led to the mandate of 4 June where Indian politics once again appeared to be regaining its organized footing, before coming to any conclusions.

Silent Crossover

Amidst BJP's roars of '*400 paar*', the opposition alliance that from the outside looked like a motley crew, but which was glued together by its desire to defeat the NDA, continued to repeatedly warn the country of how the BJP wanted a thumping mandate to amend the Constitution, weaken democratic institutions and focus on Hindu nationalism while 'othering' the country's minorities. The argument, however, was largely dismissed by political analysts, terming it as weak and stating that it lacked connection with the populace.

However, unknown to many, amidst the clamour of '*Jai Shri Ram*' and '*Bharat Mata ki Jai*', a quiet space had begun to form for this new narrative—one so subtle that its presence was barely perceptible.

During the coverage of the elections, we happened to be in Bermo, about 100 kilometres from Ranchi, the capital of Jharkhand. It was here that conversations with some young men from tribal communities threw up this perspective. Bipul Hembrom, a twenty-eight-year-old local youth, was of the opinion that no political party should be so powerful as to affect the rights or entitlements of the common people. He believed that in a strong democracy, no entity should be overly dominant, advocating for continual change. While he didn't have specific grievances against the central government or the BJP, he felt that the government had become somewhat aloof. According to him, his community, or any sensible person for that matter, will not favour bullying tactics. His reference was to the incarceration of former Chief Minister Hemant Soren on corruption charges in their state, which he considered unjust. Their group did not identify themselves as supporters of any political party and had previously voted for the BJP but believed that a strong Opposition was essential for the country, regardless of who was in power. They also emphasized that no administration should wield excessive power, pointing out the need for the public to keep them in check.

For this group, issues like the Ram Mandir or nationalism did not hold as much importance. In fact, they were also critical of the mainstream media, who they believed had neglected important issues. They raised pertinent questions about whether discussing essential issues that concerned the citizens would amount to neglecting Hinduism. One youth in a somewhat agitated tone even went as far as to question what good religion or patriotism could do, if as citizens they couldn't secure their rights. He went on to ask if this country was indeed truly committed to providing significant opportunities and respect to its large population groups.

The sentiments echoed in Bermo were not isolated, but one that found resonance across various regions, albeit subtly. Slowly but surely there seemed to be a visible fatigue about the ubiquitous reference to Hindutva and nationalism. A sizeable population also began to indicate that they did not believe that Hindus were in danger as was being projected all this while, and that issues related to their community, their caste, their livelihood were more prevalent in their minds.

The mood of the nation was visible as we took a fifty-one-hour-long train journey from Delhi to Thiruvananthapuram on the Kerala Express, just hours ahead of the first phase of the seven-phase polling. As many as 18 million Indians commute by train every single day. It is often said that a railway bogie is a microcosm of India. It sure did turn out to be one as I was brought face to face with the issues that were at the top of the mind of the electorate.

Our first interaction, as we began the journey, was with a fellow passenger in the next berth. Thirty-year-old Akanksha Nigam, a PhD scholar from Almora University and a civil services aspirant, immediately pointed out that her biggest concern at that time was the paper leaks issue during the public examinations. Fifty-three-year-old Anand Sunderrajan, a tourist guide working in Madurai, was concerned about equal opportunities for people of all castes and communities, including the minor tribal groups. While he admitted that his life had changed post the consecration of Ram Temple in Ayodhya and the inauguration of the Kashi Vishwanath Corridor in Varanasi, as the footfall of tourists had increased, he felt BJP's margin of victory could go down in Varanasi.

Twenty-five-year-old Vineet Kumar who works as a technician with the Indian railways and was travelling from Kanpur to his workstation in a carriage factory in Tirupati, talked about the dearth of jobs. '*Youth ke liye job bahot bada issue hai* (It is a huge issue for the youth),' he said. He pointed out that railways had announced no vacancies for technicians and loco pilots over the last five years. He also pointed out that 5000 (other) vacancies had been announced, while the number should have been 35,000. Speaking further on the issue of the Ram Temple, he matter-of-factly mentioned that while the establishment of the temple was good, it was about time creation of medical facilities received a similar impetus.

Hiraman Nishad, thirty-six, who belonged to Maharajganj in Uttar Pradesh and worked as a gas cutter, sounded a concluding word of caution by saying, '*Loktantr hai kab mat phir jaye pata nahi. Ye janta ka faisla hai . . . 2012 mein Mayawati aayi thi UP mein lekin usko badalne mein janta ne waqt nahin lagaya . . . janta faisla legi* (In a democracy, the will of people prevails. In 2012 Mayawati rose to power in UP, but the people turned the mandate around. People will decide).'

What one couldn't miss was that there was a clear shift in thinking from being sentiment-based to being issue-based. This truly was a major spin in the country's politics, one in which BJP found itself entangled. What was also evident was that while the Modi brand remained strong, the influence of the BJP and its leaders at the local level was waning.

We had asked the prime minister about the heavy dependence on the Modi brand in every seat, during our interview with him. He had gone on to dismiss this accusation, stating that this was a falsehood spread by dynastic parties.

The BJP operates like a team, with each member of the team working tirelessly, he had stated emphatically. 'In our party, every leader and worker are assigned a responsibility. I ask, are our party's national presidents not conducting rallies every day? Are our ministers, chief ministers and party officials not holding road shows and rallies? As prime minister, I connect with people, but people connect with us through our MP candidates. Our MP candidates promise to fulfil local aspirations while I carry a national vision to the people. The importance of our candidates is as crucial as connecting people with the idea of a developed India. Our entire team is committed to securing every seat for the lotus symbol,' he had said.

With issues like employment and inflation scoring over emotional issues, we had also asked PM Modi what his plans were for the youth in the first 100 days after winning. 'Would you like to assure the youth on the issue of employment?' we had asked specifically. He indicated that there was a great need to address employment, and that they had prepared 'an action plan for the first 100 days of the government, allocating twenty-five days specifically for the youth'. He also mentioned that in the last ten years, they had successfully controlled the inflation rate. 'Today, the world is facing a warlike situation in different corners. The impact of these circumstances has affected the country's economy and inflation. We have given priority to the interests of our people in front of powerful countries of the world and have not allowed the prices of petrol and diesel to increase. If the prices of petrol and diesel increase, everything becomes expensive,' he had asserted.

As the results poured in, however, it was clear to see that these issues had an impact. The fact was that while Ram Mandir had emerged as the mega electoral plank of the BJP, its electoral utility had possibly worn off.

On the other hand, with promises like 30 lakh government jobs and monthly salary deposits for women, which were highlighted by the Opposition, BJP's pitch on Hindutva and nationalism was weakened.

Interestingly, the Opposition also didn't seem to grasp this sentiment in its entirety. In fact, a senior opposition leader revealed on conditions of anonymity that they had largely given up hope this time around, leading them to refrain from deploying extensive resources for the elections. However, as the first phase of elections approached, they were pleasantly surprised by the positive feedback from people.

Getting back to the subject of the mandate being used to rewrite the Constitution, while covering elections in Maharashtra, we interviewed Chhagan Bhujbal, a senior leader from the Mahayuti alliance in Nashik. On the Opposition's charge that the NDA is seeking 400 seats because it wants to amend the Constitution and whether the 'ab ki baar 400 paar' slogan has hurt the NDA alliance, Bhujbal said, 'The Opposition's campaign on this has been a strong one. People think the slogan is about changing the Constitution. And a BJP MP in Karnataka (Anantkumar Hegde) had also said this.'[2]

He added, 'PM Modi has, however, said several times that the Constitution is strong, and it can't be changed even by B.R. Ambedkar himself. But this message is being given to the people. The impact will be seen only when the ballot boxes are opened.'

When the ballot boxes were opened, it was indeed found that the narrative had slowly but surely found resonance, particularly among the country's impoverished population.

Phir Teri Kahani Yaad Aae

Another aspect that perhaps led to the decline of the political dividends of Hindutva and nationalistic politics was what has been popularly referred to as the resurgence of the Mandal–Kamandal politics, in its 2.0 avatar.

In the 1990s, the Mandal Commission's recommendations on reservations had led to significant political and social upheaval. This period had seen the rise of caste-based politics and witnessed a challenge to the dominance of upper-caste Hindus. In fact, after years of dominance of the upper castes in power, the Mandal era saw a shift of power towards the backward classes. So much so that riding on the Mandal chariot, leaders like Laloo Prasad Yadav, Nitish Kumar, Mulayam Singh Yadav and Mayawati, among others, had been able to throw a spanner in the works of the BJP which had brought command politics to the forefront, with the demolition of the Babri Masjid in Ayodhya in 1992 and the rise of religious politics in the name of Lord Ram.

The Mandal vs Kamandal politics of yesteryears provided a historical context to a new narrative subsequently. After the establishment of the Ram Temple, when the BJP was confident of a comfortable win riding the Hindutva wave, the Opposition countered it with its own social engineering reminiscent of the Mandal politics. For one, there was an attempt to resurrect identity politics by invoking a demand for the caste census, which the Opposition believed had the potential to deny Modi a third term as prime minister. Leaders like Akhilesh Yadav, Hemant Soren, Sharad Pawar, Uddhav Thackeray and Tejashwi Yadav also employed social engineering in ticket distribution, a strategy that went on to show clear benefits.

The Opposition also did not let go of any opportunity to question PM Modi on seeking votes in the name of religion. 'Why are you (PM Modi) asking for votes on the basis of mangalsutra, *bhains*, and religion? Why doesn't PM Modi tell the people what work he has done in the past ten years?' Priyanka Gandhi Vadra had emphatically asked.[3]

In fact, in our interview with Priyanka Gandhi Vadra, she very vocally stated that BJP's thoughts on the issues of nationalism and Hindutva are hollow. 'Using religion for political gain and spreading division in society is unjust,' she had said. She had gone on to add that she didn't 'need to counter them on religion and nationalism'.

She added, 'Members of my family have shed their blood for this country. We don't need certificates of patriotism from BJP leaders. Nor will we ever need them. A leader's religion is serving the people. We will fulfil this duty lifelong.'

Impact of Alternative Media

The 2024 General Elections went on to shatter several myths as also reveal some interesting trends. An important one being the emergence of an alternative media which succeeded in crafting a narrative parallel to the state-centric one. In fact, the 2024 General Elections will go down in history as it saw the coming of age of opposition parties in terms of leveraging alternative media. Social media, in fact, created avenues for alternative viewpoints and helped voice a cognitive dissonance with the government narrative. The INDIA bloc, in particular, utilized social media to voice their dissent against mainstream media. Rahul Gandhi, for one, notably abstained from mass media interviews, relying instead on digital platforms to convey his messages.

In our interview with Priyanka Gandhi Vadra, she accused the mainstream media of promoting the BJP's narrative and keeping the public away from real issues. She went on to say, 'In this election, the public has started to see the reality of the government and the media . . . The public sees that TV and media are creating another image of the Modi government, but the reality is that youth are struggling with terrible unemployment, people are suffering from inflation. Increasing taxes on the middle class, increasing EMI, is a blow. BJP, which sat in power for ten years, did not listen to the people on these issues, nor did anything. The public wanted to hear about their issues in the elections, but BJP talked about things like buffalo, mangalsutra, and water theft from pipelines. The Congress Party, INDIA bloc, talked about the people's issues,' she asserted.

As mainstream media in India grappled with accusations of bias, independent digital media platforms filled the void, becoming trusted sources of information and agents of change. Key influencers like Dhruv Rathee produced viral videos criticizing the BJP, garnering millions of views among the youth. These videos played a crucial role in shaping public opinion, highlighting issues ranging from constitutional changes to youth unemployment. Speaking of the power of alternative media, Rajya Sabha MP Derek O'Brien stated, 'It's putting power in the voter's hands, literally! The mobile phone has become the most potent election weapon—the ultimate medium of outreach and empowerment. That India has the biggest national YouTube audience—46 crore people—is, in a sense, an indictment of the country's formal or "Legacy Media" landscape and its fading credibility.' Speaking of alternate media, he goes on to add that the technology may be rudimentary, 'It could even mean shooting or recording videos on mobile phones. But the uptake has been fascinating. The disintermediation of political communication, reaching voters directly and bypassing distrusted go-betweens, is exciting.'[4]

While the BJP initially dismissed this shift, as the results unfolded, they went on to prove beyond doubt that these platforms were indeed consequential, particularly among first-time voters. It was observed that brand Rahul Gandhi also strengthened significantly compared to previous years.

India Shining Once Again?

Several analysts as well as opposition leaders have also held up BJP's '*400 paar*' campaign as an example of their complacency and overconfidence. In many ways the '*400 paar*' campaign is being seen as a repeat of the 'India Shining' phenomenon. The reference being to how the Vajpayee government had been taken by surprise back in 2004 when they had even advanced the General Elections in the anticipation of a win buoyed by several factors. India, at the time, had not only won the Kargil War, but also the GDP growth rate was as high as 8.4 per cent in the second quarter of 2003; India's foreign reserves were on an upswing and Vajpayee's popularity was on a high. As for the Opposition, it had lost assembly polls in Rajasthan, Madhya Pradesh and Chhattisgarh. Vajpayee's government therefore ran a (over)confident 'India Shining' campaign which has been often talked about, albeit not for the reasons it was intended. In line with the overall mood, the exit polls also predicted a comfortable win for the NDA. As the results poured in, however, the pre-poll alliances of the BJP-led NDA and the Congress-led United Progressive Alliance (UPA) had won 181 and 218 seats, respectively. Clearly the government had failed to take into account the many issues that were plaguing India at the ground level.

The year 2024 played out somewhat similarly. This time around though the BJP under PM Modi wasn't perceived as overconfident; the prime minister himself clocked over 200 rallies and about eighty interviews, criss-crossing the entire country with roadshows and public meetings. The same, however, could not be said of the state cadres. Internal differences and fights in these cadres played out in full public view as they believed in the 400-plus slogan and set out to settle scores against each other.

At the macro level, while India's low inflation and high growth were being held up amidst the global gloom, the persisting depression in demand in the hinterland hadn't been taken into account. Lack of jobs and inequality as the underbelly of the shining economy was perhaps missed or airbrushed, but it raised its head with the election results.

To Sum Up

A unique aspect of the 2024 election results, one that also led to a virtual meme fest on social media, was that both the BJP-led NDA as well as the INDIA bloc projected the outcome as victory for themselves. If on the one hand, Narendra Modi returning as the prime minister for the third straight term, equalling Nehru's record was a cause of celebration for the NDA, INDIA bloc saw the mandate differently. Congress MP Rahul Gandhi said that 'the main message in this election is that people have unanimously and clearly said, "we don't want Narendra Modi and Amit Shah involved in the running of this country".[5]

The fact, however, is that the result presented bouquets and brickbats for each side.

For one, analysts have pointed out how excessive reliance on brand Modi to deliver the election victory may have overwhelmed the BJP. That it also led to the party machinery riding roughshod over local considerations in the choice of candidates, led the party to its poor performance. The bigger fear, however, is that the party may no longer have its ear to the ground as it once did, especially since it seemed to be caught off guard in the three most populous states in India: Uttar Pradesh, Maharashtra and West Bengal. In West Bengal, for instance, the exit polls had predicted[6] a sweeping victory for the BJP, driven by their aggressive campaign against Chief Minister Mamata Banerjee who, despite being part of the INDIA bloc, continued to be an unattached member and didn't go for an alliance in the state with the Congress and the Left. In the run-up to the polls, PM Modi had visited the state more than seven times in two months, inaugurating development projects, laying foundation stones and holding roadshows. All of this was driven by the fact that West Bengal, along with other eastern states, was supposed to play a crucial role in BJP's mission of securing 400-plus seats. The run-up to the elections also saw several dramatic developments in West Bengal. One of them was the quitting of a judge of Calcutta High Court, Justice Abhijit Gangopadhyay, who had run-ins with the ruling Trinamool Congress in the state. Hours later, he confirmed he will join the BJP. In an interview to us, Abhijit Gangopadhyay had said that his 'resignation was a result of the insulting remarks by Trinamool persons against him'. He went on to say, 'When I was trying to do justice as I was exploring and discovering huge corruption in education appointments—schoolteachers and employees in different schools in the state, they challenged me to come to politics, so I started thinking . . . now the time has come to stand beside the large number of helpless people of our state.' Gangopadhyay not only went on to contest from Tamluk constituency but also won with a convincing margin of 77,733 votes. If Gangopadhyay's political gamble yielded results, a big symbolic fight which the BJP went on to lose was in Bashirhat. The Sandeshkhali residents' allegations of land grab, extortion and sexual harassment against Trinamool leader Sheikh Shahjahan, presently in Enforcement Directorate custody, had emerged as a key talking point for the Lok Sabha election. The BJP, in order to further drive in the narrative, fielded Rekha Patra, an alleged victim. While the BJP projected Rekha Patra as the 'Shakti Swaroopa who had sent powerful people to jail', she went on to lose Basirhat to TMC's Haji Nurul Islam. Win or loss in individual seats apart, BJP went on to lose Bengal, garnering all of twelve seats as opposed to the TMC's twenty-nine.

Similarly, even before India went to the polls, Uttar Pradesh was being touted as its biggest win—a large state that sends the largest chunk of legislators to the Parliament.

In 2014 and 2019, the state had in fact made the BJP's fortunes. This time around, the BJP, however, failed to read the mood of the electorate correctly. With the Opposition claiming that the BJP could take away constitutional rights of historically disadvantaged communities such as Dalits, the BJP ended with just thirty-three seats. Interestingly BJP's loss in UP included the Faizabad constituency, which includes Ayodhya, the site of the Ram Temple that was projected as a big win for the Hindu community led by Modi. A big win for the Congress was also the seat of Amethi, where K.L. Sharma of the Congress drubbed Union Minister Smriti Irani by a handsome margin. Amethi had earlier been in the news when the BJP had slammed the Congress for fielding Rahul Gandhi from Raebareli instead of Amethi constituency, stating that the grand old party has given up its hopes on winning Amethi. Gandhi had lost the seat to Irani in the 2019 Lok Sabha election. The year 2024, however, did not turn out to be an encore, and how.

The UP result, along with losses in Maharashtra, was instrumental in the BJP being short of a majority on its own, forcing them to rely on alliance partners to form a government.

While regional issues played an important part, a major aspect of the 2024 elections that deserves a re-mention was also that the Constitution became an unexpectedly significant factor, with the Opposition claiming that its rewriting could eliminate reservations. A claim that took on a life of its own, impacting the results.

What does all of this, however, mean in the context of poll planks in the future? Does it mean that issues of Hindutva or nationalism won't work any more? Will these topics take a back seat in Indian politics? Will the Indian voter continue to vote for constitutional values? Will democratic aspects of parliamentary politics trump majoritarian agenda?

These questions need careful consideration. Reaching a conclusion too hastily, however, would be premature.

What can be said, though, is that going forward, the BJP's future strategies would likely involve reinforcing their core narrative while addressing the rising concerns of social justice and economic disparity. The Opposition, on the other hand, would need to sustain and strengthen their new narrative to remain relevant and competitive in the Indian political scenario.

Chapter 1

JNU: Split Down the Middle

February 2016

Scene 1

A WhatsApp group of forty-somethings, all friends from school and now well-placed professionals

Ravi: (After spending millions from the taxpayers' pockets, what JNU (Jawaharlal Nehru University) finally produces are budding terrorists #ShutdownJNU

Ritika: I couldn't agree more. It has only bred anti-nationals and their sympathizers.

Arjun: There are about 900 universities in India but there is no such trouble anywhere except in two or three of them—JNU, AMU (Aligarh Muslim University), Jamia Milia Islamia. Every university produces luminaries, but these three universities produce more goons.

This WhatsApp group is demonstrative of the popular outpourings and messages that were in circulation during these events. The participants in the chat are fictional. Any similarity to actual persons, living or dead, is purely coincidental.

Vishal: One needs to probe into who is funding them. Is it China? Pakistan?

Rohan: Guys, guys! Aren't you all jumping the gun? Isn't there a right to dissent in our democracy? #StandWithJNU

Ravi: Didn't think we had an anti-national among us also.

Ritika: Am shocked too. Looks like the Tukde Tukde Gang has its members spread wide.

A vigorous argument follows with links and counter-links to articles.

Rohan: It's pointless talking to you guys.

Rohan left

Scene 2

A cab on the streets of Delhi navigating protesting students who had spilled on to the road outside the JNU campus

Cab driver (*breaking the silence*): *Iss university ko band kar dena chahiye* (This university should be shut down).

Passenger: *Kyun* [Why]?

Cabbie (*pointing to some WhatsApp forwards on his phone*): *Ye dekhiye sahab, ye log kaise gorment ke paise waste kar rahe hain. Ganja aur pata nahi kya kya peete hain. Students hain toh inhe kya zaroorat hai Kashmir ke mudde mein ghusne ki* (These boys and girls are wasting the government's money. They smoke weed and do all sorts of things. Why do students have to meddle in the affairs of Kashmir?)

* * *

The Country without a Post Office

Things started heating up on a chilly evening in February 2016 on the sprawling campus of JNU in New Delhi, where a protest was to be organized against what the protesters called the 'judicial killing' of the 2001 Parliament attack convict Afzal Guru and Kashmiri separatist Maqbool Bhat, and in solidarity with 'the struggle of Kashmiri people for their democratic right to self-determination'.[1] Drawing reference from a collection of poems written by the Kashmiri–American poet Agha Shahid Ali, the event, titled *The Country Without a Post Office*, was to be a 'cultural evening' with poetry, music and art.

Only, no one knew at the time that this seat of higher learning was soon to acquire a dubious distinction—that of becoming one of the most polarizing metaphors in Indian politics in recent times. Overnight, its students would go from being research scholars to 'jihadis', 'violent communists' and 'anti-nationals'. If social media conversations that would soon surface were to be believed, JNU was filled with 'traitors' who were a 'blot on Indian democracy', a 'taxpayer's burden' and who spent their time 'inciting violent uprisings'. Not just that, typing keywords such as 'anti-national', 'sedition', 'patriotism' as also *'Bharat Mata ki Jai'* on Google maps would direct users to the now (ill) famed Jawaharlal Nehru University.[2]

The soaring rhetoric around JNU would not just be limited to polity but would also threaten to disrupt filial relationships, both in the physical world and on that other staple of Indian life—family WhatsApp groups. History would record JNU as being one of those instruments that would draw battle lines across blood lines. Come to think of it, disagreements about politics have been the staple diet of every family get-together, except that the split caused this time would lead to relationships caving under pressure, giving new meaning to 'social distancing', which was to become the way of the physical world in a few years.

With Akhil Bharatiya Vidyarthi Parishad (ABVP), a BJP- and Rashtriya Swayamsevak Sangh (RSS)-supported student organization, alleging that anti-India slogans were raised at the event, and after media outlets began airing videos of the students several nights in a row, purportedly shouting '*azadi*', an FIR was filed against several JNU students, including the then JNU Students' Union president, Kanhaiya Kumar. Four days after the initial event, national rhetoric was at its peak when the Delhi Police arrested Kanhaiya Kumar on charges of sedition and criminal conspiracy under Section 124 of the Indian Penal Code, which dates back to 1860. Such was the collective frenzy around the case that when Kumar was produced in court on 16 February 2016, he was assaulted by a group of lawyers who also beat up journalists, professors and students on the premises.

It was almost as if one were staring at two irreconcilable understandings of India—one that the tension-filled relationship between JNU and the ruling government stood for. Not only had the institution traditionally been known to be the government's bugbear, but things had come to a head earlier that year when JNU had been vociferous in its protests following the death of Rohith Vemula, a Dalit student at Hyderabad University who had committed suicide after allegedly being targeted by the campus administration, which was seen as being supportive of ABVP. This time, though, with the sedition row, JNU had ended up making a huge offering to the government, albeit unwittingly.

Just two years earlier, in the 2014 General Elections, the BJP had run a high-adrenalin campaign, with its leader being positioned as a *Hindu Hriday Samrat* (King of the Hindu Hearts). The power of the political narrative, social engineering and the 'subaltern Hindutva' ideological consolidation of the BJP-Sangh *parivar* had led the party to its unprecedented victory. Immediately after the General Elections, however, the BJP went on to lose the Delhi and Bihar state assembly elections. In fact, the 2015 Bihar elections led to a winning electoral arithmetic for the *Mahagathbandhan* or Grand Alliance of the Janata Dal (United) (JDU) and the Rashtriya Janata Dal (RJD). Clearly, the arithmetic of caste had won over the overarching theme of Hindutva. Meanwhile, there was another arithmetic playing out in the national capital of Delhi where the AAP had secured a landslide victory based on its '*aam admi*' or common man appeal. It was clear that the electorate was willing to experiment with different parties in the state and at the Centre. While the BJP had invoked Babasaheb Ambedkar as a nationalist icon, popular opinion was that it had used Ambedkar only as a symbolic artefact, while 'othering' the Dalits at the social level. The Rohith Vemula case was also being showcased to point out that despite its talk of inclusive Hindutva, the BJP lacked accountability regarding the social and political concerns of the Dalits.

For the BJP, it was clearly time to change the political discourse; it was widely believed that the party needed something beyond Hindutva to help reinforce its charisma, which was fast fading. An opportunity fell into their lap with JNU. To put it in perspective, not only did JNU come as a shot in the arm for the BJP, importantly, it would also go on to give the party an opportunity to win back the support of the youth irrespective of their caste affiliations. The nationalism plank, which the BJP now wore on its sleeve, would go on to become an even greater unifying force than Hindutva and would emerge as the BJP's strongest weapon in times to come.

A Decisive Phone Call

If the BJP was in a hurry to turn their fortunes with the JNU opportunity, the Opposition didn't want to waste any time either in playing catch. On 13 February 2016, when the vice president of the Congress Party, Rahul Gandhi, was on his way back from an event, he received a phone call that would completely change the colour of the student protest at JNU. The phone call was from the Communist Party of India (Marxist) (CPI[M]) supremo, Sitaram Yechury, himself a JNU alumnus, to request Gandhi's participation in the ongoing student protests at JNU. While sources tell us that there were differing opinions within the Congress Party about getting involved in what was still being seen as a student protest, Rahul Gandhi made up his mind to make an appearance at JNU on that very day and contribute to the narrative of the developments at JNU being a 'political conspiracy' by the Centre to terrorize the students.

'A youngster expressed himself and the government says he is an anti-national. The most anti-national people are the people that are suppressing the voice of that institution,' Gandhi reportedly told students.[3] The battle lines were clearly drawn. In response to Gandhi's remark, 'It seems only the Bharatiya Janata Party and the Rashtriya Swayamsevak Sangh have the licence to say who is a traitor and who is a patriot.'[4] Amit Shah accused Gandhi of being unable to draw the distinction between pro-national and anti-national activities and asked him to apologize to the nation in a blog titled 'Is this Congress' new definition of nationalism'.[5] The high-decibel attack even led some members within the

Congress Party to feel that this incident had weakened the party in the face of BJP's nationalism narrative. On one side, five years later, Kanhaiya Kumar, the key protagonist in the JNU event, would go on to join the Congress soon and would contest the 2024 Lok Sabha Polls as a Congress candidate from North East Delhi.

The morning of 14 February 2016, the day after Rahul Gandhi's visit to JNU, saw the BJP upping the ante further with Home Minister Rajnath Singh making a statement that the JNU incident was supported by the Lashkar-e-Taiba (LeT) chief, Hafiz Saeed. Not just that, the BJP decided to follow this up with a Jan Swabhiman Abhiyan (people's campaign for self-respect) from 18 to 20 February to stir up 'nationalism' among countrymen to counter the threat of 'separatism' and 'political conspiracy'.

'BJP strategizing to take nationalism debate to masses'— thus ran the headlines of most major dailies on 17 February. Meanwhile, an *Economic Times* report deconstructed BJP's strategy for the Jan Swabhiman Abhiyan, writing 'The nationalism issue has not just enthused the BJP but also Sangh fountainhead RSS and a roadmap for wooing the people towards it in the name of patriotism is being prepared, sources said.'[6]

'BJP will also slam the Congress for its "anti-India" stance and policies in this campaign,' the same report went on to add.

More than a Varsity at War

Overall, it was clear that it was no longer just a varsity at war; what so far had been a campus row was now being leveraged to split the country down the middle, leaving the nation divided. To quote Professor Makarand R. Paranjape, professor of

English at JNU, 'JNU became a microcosm, a theatre where
the opposing sides of the Nationalism debate clashed.' On the
one side was the government and a section of people who called
the students anti-nationals, terrorists, jihadis, pro-Pakistanis,
and on the other were the teachers, students and a wide range
of artists who saw this as a university crackdown. Not only
did JNU become a fault line in Indian politics, the sedition
row in JNU also became the catalyst for anger against student
movements at large.

'How could students be so anti-national—that was the
question that even Uber drivers started asking me when I put
JNU as my pick up or drop point,' reminisces Professor Paranjape.

This wasn't the first time, though, that JNU had come
under attack for being 'anti-national'. Even before the
crackdown on JNU, an article in *Panchjanya* magazine,
which is published by the RSS, had pronounced that JNU
is home to 'a huge anti-national block which has the aim of
disintegrating India'.[7]

After the JNU saga, which sparked debates over nationalism
and free speech, a BJP MLA spoke of 3000 condoms being
found in the dustbins of JNU while prime-time television
debates focused on the university's 'anti-national' DNA.

'As a student leader, we had students coming to us every
day whose landlords had called them traitors,' recounts Mohit
Kumar Pandey, former president of the JNU Students' Union.
'The label of anti-national was quite strange, as through it
questions were raised about various things,' he adds. 'After the
JNU condom incident, a female student recounted how someone
commented on her clothes and said it was because of the kind
of clothes she wore that she engaged in anti-national activities.
I was surprised at the association of women's clothing with
anti-national activities,' he says, part amused, part repulsed. His
own tryst with the anti-national moniker with an autorickshaw

driver, he recalls, led him to convincing the auto driver to come and visit the iconic Ganga Dhaba on campus. 'The auto driver was served tea as he interacted with the students. I distinctly recall the driver's exact words as he was about to leave; he said, "Brother, I didn't find any traitor here." But that didn't matter any more, as the branding of the university as a hub of anti-national activities was complete.'

Speaking of the extent of the attack, Pandey remembers walking to a shop in the neighbouring Ber Sarai area one day, from where they often got posters printed, only to find it shut. 'On spending a considerable time inquiring, I found out with much difficulty that the shop owner was taken away by the special cell of the Delhi Police. For good measure, strict instructions were given not to mention this incident in the media or even to tell any JNU student about it. I was taken aback; to think that posters were considered such a significant tool for expression that their messenger was being shot was too much to fathom. Till date, even though the guy has never revealed what questioning he had to undergo or even how his release finally happened, I end up thinking a lot about his ordeal. What was his crime—that he printed posters for JNU?'

That or perhaps the messenger was deemed to be a part of the 'Tukde Tukde Gang'—one of the several additions to the popular lexicon that drew on the allegation that JNU students had chanted slogans about dividing India into fragments. The contempt towards the so-called urban progressives also found expression through a variety of other descriptors and monikers such as 'urban Naxals'. This new terminology gained vast popularity via both mass media and social media. It will be worthwhile to remember that this was a time when terms like 'libtards' were already doing the global rounds, and in India too, the pseudo-secular had resorted to toxic name-calling made legit by social media. If there were cries of 'sickular' on the one end, you were quick to be labelled a 'bhakt' on the other end of the divide. Interestingly, the new phrases that were added to the lexicon, which were coined in TV studios, went on to have an afterlife of their own, propelled as much by the common people as by the ruling elite and soon even turning into official speak. At a much later date, officials in the Union home ministry would find themselves at their wits, end over an RTI application that sought details of members who were part of the oft-proclaimed 'Tukde Tukde Gang', a term that had been used umpteen times by Prime Minister Narendra Modi and Union Home Minister Amit Shah. The RTI reply query, several years after the JNU incident, led the ministry of home affairs to admit, on record, that it had 'no information' concerning the 'Tukde Tukde Gang'.[8] But we digress.

David vs Goliath

Coming back to the JNU incident, amidst the polarization between 'us' the nationalists and 'them' the anti-nationals, came Kanhaiya Kumar's release, all guns blazing. With forensic analysis by investigating agencies revealing that the video that showed the anti-national slogans being raised had been doctored, what followed was Kumar's interim bail and his rousing reception at JNU. Kumar's fiery speech, which was beamed live on just about every news channel, spoke of an extremely partisan administration that brooked no criticism. '*Ladke lenge,*' Kumar shouted, grinning at the crowd gathered at the JNU administrative block. '*Azadi,*' the crowd responded to his clarion call. They were demanding 'azadi' in India and not from India, Kumar clarified. 'Kanhaiya's victorious return to JNU was something quite out of this world. Can you blame his admirers for thinking that revolution was just around the corner?' says Professor Paranjape, who witnessed the event first-hand. The only parallel in terms of alternative politics was Anna Hazare's tumultuous rally at the Ramlila Maidan, feels Paranjape. 'The singing, dancing and swaying of the crowds to the slogans of Azadi cannot be imagined today,' he goes on to add.

It was the archetypal David taking on Goliath moment as Kanhaiya did not let his listeners forget for an instant that he belonged to a poverty-stricken family, and that JNU had provided him and several others an opportunity for social mobility. His speech did not leave any stone unturned in projecting a battle between the powerless and the powerful.

The defining images of Kanhaiya Kumar leading students to raise the infectious chant of 'azadi' after his release did put BJP on the back foot but only temporarily. The stakes were too high for the BJP as they simply could not afford that the focus shift from the 'anti-nationalism' plank, especially given the upcoming elections in states such as West Bengal and Assam, where illegal immigration and the changing demographic profile were key poll issues. It was no coincidence also that the RSS chief, Mohan Bhagwat, chose the backdrop of the JNU row over anti-national slogans to affirm that everyone should be taught to chant '*Bharat Mata ki Jai*', the catchphrase becoming yet another test to judge a person's patriotism and claim to being a true nationalist.

JNU, of course, would once again be in the news a few years later, when a masked mob, armed with iron rods and sticks, would enter the campus spreading chaos and terror in a three-hour rampage as they chanted *Jai Shri Ram*'. The mob attack was reported hours before an event in Mumbai hosted by Union Minister Piyush Goyal and BJP Vice President Baijayant Jay Panda to discuss 'myths and realities' linked to the CAA. This time, the social media frenzy following the incident was exacerbated when an A-lister Bollywood star decided to stand with the protesters, albeit silently. Familiar supporters of Modi's government would go on to deride Deepika Padukone, accusing her of mining publicity for her new film, *Chhapaak*, through her JNU appearance. On Twitter, once again rival hashtags asking people to both support and boycott her new film would begin to trend, as was now common; the mob attack trumped by the new controversy.

Mandal–Kamandal Politics

To put things in perspective, the JNU incident cannot lay claim to pioneering jingoism or proclaiming people and events as being 'anti-national'. Not long before, Mandal politics had given legitimacy to populist politics, even as a section had described demanding reservations for Other Backward Castes (OBCs) and implementing the Mandal Commission report as being 'anti-national'.[9]

It was at this time that the BJP leader Lal Krishna Advani came up with the perfect foil for the Mandal agitation—the kamandal politics of Hindutva—which preached hyper-nationalism as well as harped on Hindu solidarity and the need to unite all Hindus to oppose the Mandal Commission's recommendation of reservations for OBCs. The new language of Hindutva pride, and by far the biggest mass mobilization of Hindutva forces, then played out in the form of the famous 'Rath Yatra' or chariot procession, which covered 10,000 kilometres and passed through ten states to support the agitation of the Vishwa Hindu Parishad and its affiliates to erect a temple on the site of the Babri Masjid.

Come to think of it, zealous sloganeering and rhetoric are not new to the political landscape either. In 1993, for instance, the BJP, in light of its Ram Temple movement, tried to mobilize mass support with, *'Baccha baccha Ram ka janam bhoomi ke kaam ka'*, urging every child of Ram to stand up for the cause of building the Ram Temple at the site of the Babri Masjid. Only at the time, the 'hurt sentiments' gallery didn't really play out as extensively as in the current times, as is evident in the fact that the Samajwadi Party–Bahujan Samaj Party (SP–BSP) combine made inroads into every region of Uttar Pradesh with its counter of *'Mile Mulayam Kanshiram, hawa mein ud gaye Jai Shri Ram'*, implying that the Mulayam Singh–Kanshi Ram combine was enough to defeat BJP despite its invocation of Lord Ram.

What the JNU incident can lay claim to, though, is ensuring that nationalism as a concept became so ingrained in the response system that it came to define modern Indian lifestyles. From standing up for the national anthem as a measure of one's patriotism before one as much as watched a film in a theatre, to the overarching debate around who is a true nationalist, every aspect of life was revisited, as it were. 'According to me, the JNU incident of 2016 marked a crucial turning point in India's political discourse, especially among the youth,' says social historian Badri Narayan. 'Subsequent to the JNU incident, the issue of nationalism gained stronger traction. This allowed it to expand further, contributing to the intertwining of religion and nationalism in politics. This evolution led to a more aggressive and forthright political rhetoric from the outset, with assertions becoming increasingly assertive,' he goes on to add.

In fact, it was perhaps the first time since 1971, when Indira Gandhi contested elections after the 1971 Indo–Pakistan war on the nationalism plank, that nationalism had acquired a ubiquitous political fervour with 'anti-national' becoming an expletive liberally used in everyday banter, both on and off WhatsApp.

There have been several different theories to explain the rise of this strong nationalist sentiment. Some theorists like Professor Paranjape, who took a strong pro-nationalist stance in the lecture series that was organized at the so-called 'Freedom Square' at JNU to debate and discuss the definition of 'nationalism', credit 'the leftists' with the rise of nationalism, who, he feels, 'would squirm in their seats if they realized just how much they helped in bringing nationalism back centre stage. They wanted to bury it alive, but its return was more powerful than any ghost whom they could easily have exorcised.' Then there are others like Santosh Desai, an advertising professional and an astute social commentator, who points out in his popular newspaper column that 'the BJP' had won this 'internal war'. 'It has made it mandatory for everyone to have to fall in line with their definition of nationalism, and anyone who demurs has to pay the price.'

A lot of the nationalist sentiment also has to do with politics increasingly becoming an insidious force. Desai once again cuts to the chase when he points out that 'earlier times saw the separation of politics from cultural life as a natural part of the prevailing political ideology. This helped electoral politics, at the national level at least, stay outside the perimeter of our social lives. Politics was either the full-time pursuit of a specific set of people or it was an activity that was performed once every few years, and then forgotten about. The majority thought of themselves as being apolitical, and even took pride in that self-definition,' he adds. That has since changed as cultural issues enter the political mainstream. Add to it the fact that the presence of social media 'has exposed and amplified differences that used to be easier to ignore. Touchy subjects that might have caused discord once a year at the holiday dinner table are now ever-present thanks to social media,' adds Desai.[10]

While the impact of the JNU incident and its aftermath on the country and people's identities at large has been all-encompassing, it will be interesting to find out what the long-term impact of the incident has been on the JNU campus itself, where the row originated. If one were to believe Professor Paranjape, the impact has been 'practically forgotten'.

'The kind of student politics that drove it is over,' he says with unmissable finality. 'Campus politics is today tame, even a lame affair compared to those heady days. Perhaps it is for the better. JNU, as I have argued, should return to academics. But the clean-up has resulted in the diminution of the campus culture of dissent and free thinking. Unfortunately, right-wing student politics is also interested in creating political cadres rather than academics. So the right seems to be copying the tactics of the left more than it would care to acknowledge. But one thing is clear—whether at the faculty or the student levels, the old JNU is finished.' A staunch critic of JNU's leftist ideology, one may or may not agree with him, depending on the side of the political divide one finds oneself on, when he says, 'JNU's ideology itself was a relic of the past, a dodo, so to speak, which could neither fly nor lay eggs. Its demise was inevitable. I'm glad, in that sense, that the events of 2016 conspired to hasten its end.'

What he goes on to add, however, is telling of the overall state of our times and of the blurry lines on both sides of the divide: 'I am also sad that what has replaced it is conformist, even anti-intellectualist, even if it claims to be nationalist,' he says.

That leaves us with yet another question to ponder. Who is a true nationalist? If one were to go by Jim Garrison's proclamation in the iconic movie *JFK*, 'A patriot must always be ready to defend his country against his government.' This is a tough ask in times when loyalty towards the country and the government are used interchangeably. As is raising any questions in the nationalist/anti-national debate, especially since among the many accompaniments of patriotism is an inexplicable anger, with people assuming what academics call a 'mega identity' where political preferences become synonymous with an all-encompassing set of beliefs.

Speaking of rhetoric, Professor Amartya Sen had written *The Argumentative Indian* as a tip of the hat to India's diversity and its veritable feast of viewpoints. In today's times we face the risk of the moniker being changed to *The Rhetorical Indian*. If it didn't come with tragic consequences, it would even be mildly amusing to note that slogans like '*Bharat Mata ki Jai*' and '*Jai Shri Ram*', which were traditionally used to express reverence to the nation and a salutation to Lord Rama respectively, have been appropriated as political slogans. It is the clash between these two slogans that represents a larger battle for the soul of India. It is about time that the power of rhetoric is harnessed for the greater good of the nation, as opposed to allowing it to create deeper fissures.

As for what happened at JNU, it marked a significant turning point in Indian politics, successfully shaping a narrative of nationalism that resonated across the country. The BJP strategically capitalized on this incident, leveraging the slogans of '*Jai Shri Ram*' and '*Bharat Mata ki Jai*' to unify and energize their political base. This convergence of patriotic fervour gave BJP a distinct advantage, positioning them as the flag-bearers of a robust nationalist sentiment.

However, alongside its political gains, the JNU incident had nuanced repercussions. While it bolstered a new-found sense of nationalism, it also stirred unease among the younger, more progressive segments of society. This demographic, disenchanted with what they perceived as growing extremism, gradually distanced themselves from the dominant narrative. Over time, discontent among youth was further fuelled by various student-led movements and protests on diverse issues like Agniveer and leaked exam papers. These events served to deepen the generational divide and amplify dissent against the ruling party's policies and rhetoric.

In essence, while JNU catalysed a resurgence of nationalist discourse in India, it concurrently sowed seeds of discord among the youth, whose disillusionment would manifest in subsequent political landscapes. The interplay between these forces underscored the complexities and enduring impacts of identity politics in shaping national narratives and youth engagement in democracy.

Chapter 2

Large-Scale Protests: A New Playbook

Time: Sometime in January 2021

Place: A WhatsApp group of friends, largely residents of New Delhi

Mahesh: What is the nation coming to? As if it wasn't enough to block roads and inconvenience people, these farmers now have the audacity to replace the national flag with the Khalistan flag?

Sanjeev: Truly, this is anti-national behaviour at its worst. I do not think anyone should side with them now after what they did at the Red Fort.

Rakesh: I had been supporting the farmers' protest all through, even though I personally faced a lot of inconvenience in travelling every morning on account of them having blocked roads and set up makeshift camps, but this is something else. I am ashamed that I supported them all this while.

This WhatsApp group is demonstrative of the popular outpourings and messages that were in circulation during these events. The participants in the chat are fictional. Any similarity to actual persons, living or dead, is purely coincidental.

Arun: But was it the Khalistan flag at all? The violence, of course, is to be condemned, but I think we must get our facts right before we make these sweeping statements and brand our farmers anti-nationals.

Sooraj: I don't think after what has happened, you should be supporting them at all, Arun. It was absolute anarchy on the streets. They broke through barriers, fought with the police, overturned vehicles and worst of all, delivered a national insult. Anyone supporting them now needs to look at their own credentials.

Mahesh: It is simple, the farmers have played into the hands of the Opposition. There is no other explanation.

* * *

An Uncertain Calm

27 January 2021

Silence prevailed at the Gazipur border with the farmers' protest site looking like a pale shadow of its former self. A day earlier, amidst the Republic Day celebrations at Delhi's Red Fort, a rally had turned violent after protesting farmers—mostly from Punjab and Haryana—broke through police barricades to storm the historic Red Fort complex. Having started out as a peaceful demonstration in November 2020 against three contentious farm laws, and after as many as eleven rounds of talks between the government and farmer unions had failed to break the impasse, the protest had taken a violent turn with agitators clashing with the police. Images of the violence were coming in from different sources at breakneck speed, with the moment being increasingly likened to Trump supporters storming Capitol Hill. A barrage of social media posts soon began to claim that the protesters had taken down the Indian national flag and replaced the tricolour with the Khalistan flag. The few voices condemning the violence but clarifying that the flag was not the Khalistan flag but the Sikh religious flag with the 'khanda'—two swords—were quickly drowned. Public sentiment was turning increasingly negative; family WhatsApp groups, many of which had so far been sympathizers of the protesting farmers, had turned critics overnight. For the first time, farmers, who had always been looked upon as *annadatas*—food providers—were staring at an allegation of being 'anti-India', and of having 'played into the hands of the Opposition'.

'I was covering the farmers' protest from the first day. I used to go live on Facebook from different locations every day. Thousands of people used to watch. They would ask in the comments how they could get involved and help the protest. However, the support for the protest, which was strong at the beginning, decreased after the events of January 26. People started going back home,' says Debby Rai, a freelance video creator whose videos were keenly watched during the protest.

The Delhi Police, in a charge sheet that it would file later that year, would go on to state that there was a conspiracy to capture the Red Fort and make it the new site for farmer protests. It was alleged that the conspiracy had been hatched as early as November and December 2020, which had led to a huge increase in the purchase of tractors in Punjab and Haryana. On the other hand, a Punjab Vidhan Sabha committee that would be set up to investigate the alleged atrocities by the Delhi Police on farmers, youth and others from Punjab in the aftermath of the 26 January violence would go on to state that the melee was the result of a scheme hatched by the Delhi Police to defame the protesting farmers.

For now, the morale of the farmers who were protesting the three farm laws—Farmers' Produce Trade and Commerce (Promotion and Facilitation) Act, 2020, Farmers' (Empowerment and Protection) Agreement on Price Assurance and Farm Services Act, 2020, and the Essential Commodities (Amendment) Act, 2020—was completely shaken. The protesters were being viewed as rioters, their cause diluted, leaving those associated with the protest anxious. Farmer leader Pushpendra Singh reminisces how a young protester had walked up to him, grief writ large over his face. 'We are being labelled as anti-national in our own country and society,' he had said, with tears threatening to spill over. 'We were anxious. The continuous news on television was creating doubts. There had been several attempts to break our unity. Misleading information was spread at many levels. First, the angle of Khalistan was introduced. Then, foreign conspiracies and foreign funds were alleged. It was said that China was supporting our movement. The sole objective was to speak against our movement in society and the country, preventing common people from joining us,' Singh goes on to add.

To put things in perspective, the concerns put forth by the government couldn't be completely dismissed as propaganda. Notably, just days before the 26 January violence, the government had informed the Supreme Court that Khalistan supporters had 'infiltrated' the farmers' agitation. The concerns weren't completely unfounded. Banned Khalistani group, Sikhs for Justice, had announced a reward of USD 2.5 lakh for anyone who would hoist the Khalistani flag at the Red Fort on 26 January. Balbir Singh, a farmer leader says, 'A sinister plot began to unfold, shrouded in the complexity of political manoeuvring and emotional sentiment. As the events unfolded, it became evident that there was a much wider plan at play. The orchestrators of this plan seemed to have abundant resources and funds at their disposal, suggesting meticulous planning and a hidden agenda. The scale of their operations left everyone bewildered, questioning the true motives.'

Needless to say, a protest in India being used as an occasion by a terrorist outfit to propagate anti-India sentiments didn't work well for the protesters. The Republic Day violence in particular ran the risk of undercutting public support, to put it mildly. That the 26 January incident had become a blot on their otherwise peaceful protest was clear. Amidst all the confusion, one thing was certain. This incident would either shape the movement and ensure that it became strong, or it would completely discredit the cause and destroy its credibility.

Tears and Turnaround

28 January 2021

The day began with the Ghaziabad district magistrate issuing an eviction order under Section 133 of the Criminal Procedure Code (conditional order for removal of nuisance) to vacate the farmers' protest site at Ghazipur by midnight. The eviction of farmers was particularly imminent after the police began to dismantle the makeshift tents and sheds put up by the protesters.

Nobody knew at the time, though, that everything would change in a few hours. The evening of 28 January turned out to be defining when a seemingly imploding agitation found a new lease of life. It was the son of the mercurial farmer leader Mahendra Singh Tikait (who was credited with reviving the Bhartiya Kisan Union in the late 1980s with a string of dramatic protests against the then Congress government) who provided a new spark to the dying embers at the Ghazipur border protest site. Under siege, slapped with an eviction notice by the Uttar Pradesh government and facing arrest, Rakesh Tikait sent out an emotional appeal as he took to the stage to proclaim that theirs was a people's protest that could not be ended with guns or violence but with dialogue, one that could only happen with the government, not the police. 'I will commit suicide. We will stay put. We will not leave the spot,' Tikait said before slumping to the ground, crying. As he was seen sobbing on national television, he told reporters, 'This government wants to destroy the country's farmers. I will not let that happen. After my arrest, the government and the police want to have my farmers—who have made this agitation into a massive one—assaulted by the goons on their way back. I cannot desert them. They are my family. Farmers from across the country have pinned their hopes on us. I cannot betray them.'

In a tearful call to farmers to join him, Tikait filled up the leadership vacuum just when a cast down agitation was looking for a nerve centre to rally around. Slogans like '*Kisan ekta zindabad*', long live the unity of farmers, and '*Jai jawan, jai kisan*', hail soldiers and farmers, reverberated through the protest site on that chilly night as farmer morale surged. Tikait's words resonated far and wide and brought farmers back to the protest site, not just from his home state of Uttar Pradesh but from other states as well to show solidarity with the movement. It was only a matter of time before the highway at Ghazipur would be dotted with green and orange flags, a rare sight in the current polarized times.

A New Playbook

What had transpired at Ghazipur was much more than the revival of a protest; it was the emergence of a whole new playbook. For starters, it was clear for protesters to see that the nature of the times demanded an upfront proclamation of nationalistic credentials before putting forth any views. Having learnt this lesson the hard way, the farmers left no

stone unturned to communicate that the protests weren't
against the nation or even the ruling party but against the
controversial farm laws.

What better way to do that than to have the tiranga or
the tricolour as an integral part of every rally to proclaim their
Indianness! In fact, the movement became a new landmark
in the nationalist ownership of the tricolour. A multitude of
green-and-white caps and tricolour flags were seen planted on
tractors. Knowing that allowing politicians to get on the stage
would dilute the credibility of the protests and open the doors
for pro-government media to attack them as being politically
motivated, union leaders came to a consensus that the stage
would be a sacred place from where only farmer leaders would
speak. The farmers also went out of their way to ensure that
their sympathizers weren't seen as having any particular colour
or ideology. After what they referred to as a smear campaign to
malign their cause, farmers also stepped up their efforts to not
let their dissent be misconstrued by the media. What came to
their aid was an army of independent activists, photographers,
YouTubers   and   Instagrammers—popularly   known   as
alternative media.

What the farmers wanted to demonstrate through this new
approach was that nationalists didn't have only one hue and that
questioning the policies of the government didn't mean one was
against the nation.

Their challenges, however, were far from over as more
rhetoric would play out in multiple ways in the days that followed.

Toolkit of Controversy

3 February 2021

A significant addition to farmer support came by way of the
Swedish climate activist Greta Thunberg sharing a 'toolkit'

via a tweet, advising people on how to show solidarity for the farmers protesting against the contentious farm laws. It soon became a toolkit of controversy as the Delhi Police registered an FIR against its creators. Probing the tweet, the Delhi Police claimed that the toolkit had been created by the Poetic Justice Foundation (PJF), an alleged pro-Khalistan outfit. TV studios were replete with discussions about the 'toolkit gang' for days, with 'toolkit' emerging as a new word for 'protest planning'. The ruling BJP, in the meanwhile, accused the opposition parties of conspiring to malign India's image in the international space. 'When Dalits protested in Bhima Koregaon, they were dubbed as "urban Naxals", when Muslims protested they were dubbed as Pakistani and Jihadi, when students took to the streets they were called the *tukde tukde gang* (a group of people trying to divide the country) and anti-national,' Ajay Gudavarthy says in *Populism and Rhetoric Amidst the Farmers' Protest in India*. Critics felt that 'toolkit gang' was yet another addition to this growing verbiage.

The battle of words reached a crescendo as Prime Minister Modi, while speaking in a Parliament session in February, called the new 'breed' of agitators *'andolanjeevi'* ('professional protesters' or 'survivors of protest'), causing the Congress to waste no time in hitting back at the PM, referring to him as *'jumlajeevi'* ('survivor of rhetoric').

Amidst all the hyperbole, the resolve of the tillers to ensure the repeal of the three farm laws remained unshakable. It will be prudent to look at some data to understand the real cause of the protest against these laws, which farmers felt would leave them at the mercy of corporations. A survey done by Lokniti, Centre for the Study of Developing Societies (CSDS), among farmers in 2014 found that while agriculture was the main source of household income for as many as 79 per cent of respondents, 76 per cent of the respondents preferred to take up work other than farming with as many as 60 per cent wanting their children to migrate to and settle in a city.[1] A staggering reality revealed by data is that 84 per cent of the farmers in India are either small or marginal farmers. The findings of the CSDS survey seemed to be echoed by the recent 2021–22 Economic Survey of India, which noted that India's agriculture sector grew by just 3 per cent in 2021–22, a 35 per cent lower growth rate than the previous six-year average.[2] Above everything, the over 4 lakh farmer suicides since 1995 are a sobering reminder that Indian farmers are living a grim reality.

With the size of landholdings progressively declining, the one solution to improve their livelihoods that the farmers were holding on to was a high minimum support price, which the farm laws threatened to deregulate and privatize. Essentially, the laws allowed private corporations to purchase crops at market prices without paying taxes, as also to stockpile essential commodities in unlimited quantities, and engage in contract farming while denying farmers any legal recourse. The government's stance was that the reforms would provide farmers with more choice by giving them the option to sell directly to private companies while freeing them from the traditional wholesale *anaj mandis* or markets. The farmers, however, feared that the reforms would lower the prices for their products and remove an essential safety net. The manner in which the 2020 farm laws were adopted further gave farmers the impression that the government's ultimate goal was to transfer regulatory authority over agricultural markets from state governments to the Centre.

The crux of the problem, according to economist Vijay Sardana, was a lack of 'effective communication' between the two sides. The government, he feels, did not effectively educate the people about the defects or gaps in the current system.

In November 2020, convinced that what the government projected as a market-friendly overhaul of the agricultural laws could potentially put them out of business and destroy their livelihoods, farmers from Punjab, Haryana and Uttar Pradesh laid siege to the national capital.

'Why Aren't We Talking about This?'

The question raised by the Barbadian singer-songwriter Rihanna as she shared a CNN network article on the demonstrations with her 100-odd million followers on Twitter opened new floodgates.[3] Also to tweet her solidarity with the protesting Indian farmers was American lawyer and author Meena Harris, the niece of US Vice President Kamala Harris.

The Indian foreign ministry was quick to point out that international celebrities were making 'sensationalist' comments that were neither 'accurate nor responsible'. 'Before rushing to comment on such matters, we would urge that the facts be ascertained, and a proper understanding of the issues at hand be undertaken,' the Indian foreign ministry's advisory read.[4] That response set the tone for Bollywood bigwigs such as Ajay Devgn and Akshay Kumar as well as cricket legend Sachin Tendulkar, to name a few, to echo the Centre's call to oppose 'propaganda' against India's policies. Several others, however, construed this as paranoia. 'A government surer of itself would have ignored the tweet altogether,' the historian and commentator Ramachandra Guha pointed out, echoing the sentiments of many.

Whatever it was, one thing was certain—it was a stalemate.

Surprise Climb-Down

19 November 2021

'I apologize to the people of the country . . . we were not able to convince farmers [over the farm laws]. I'm here to declare that we have decided to repeal the three farm laws . . .' said PM Modi in a televised address to the nation on the occasion of Gurupurab, the birth anniversary of Guru Nanak Dev.

A year of suffering through inclement weather, the Covid-19 pandemic and the batons and tear gas of the police finally ended with Prime Minister Modi's announcement of the repeal of the three contentious farm laws. Until now the government had stood firm, labelling the farmers secessionists and pawns in the hands of opposition parties, and claiming they were ignorant about how the agricultural reforms would actually benefit them. The announcement therefore took many by surprise.

The government maintained that 'despite our efforts, we could not explain to some farmers (the benefits of the laws)'. The opposition parties, however, were quick to point out that the policy rollback came ahead of the crucial state elections in Uttar Pradesh and Punjab, which were scheduled to be held in early 2022, where farmers constitute an influential electoral cohort.

'After 600–700 farmers died during the year-long agitation, the prime minister is now apologizing for the laws but he has not uttered a word about martyred farmers. We will have to understand that the government decided to change its decision only after recent surveys showed that it was slipping,' Congress General Secretary Priyanka Gandhi Vadra was quoted as saying.[5] The BJP's debacle in the Punjab civic polls and Haryana by-elections was also speculated to be the reason behind the government's sudden change in mood, by critics.

A Seminal Protest

Irrespective of the reasons for the rollback (a bill to cancel the reforms was officially passed in Parliament in November 2021), the farmer's protest is seminal for several reasons. First, not only was the move hailed as a victory for farmers, but it was also a powerful example of the success of mass protests. While the BJP and its allies portrayed the movement as the exclusive concern of rich farmers and traders, it was clear that the agitation was joined by different sections of the peasantry, including workers. It is beyond doubt that the protests were the largest-ever mobilization of the peasantry in independent India. Police atrocities, if anything, only helped the cause of the movement. A viral photograph of an old Sikh farmer being threatened by a paramilitary policeman at the Singhu border, for instance, had in many ways come to define the protest. Many, including the photojournalist Ravi Choudhary, who took the picture, tagged the image with *Jai jawan, jai kisan*'—a slogan coined by former Indian prime minister Lal Bahadur Shastri in 1965 during the India–Pakistan war to stress the importance of soldiers and farmers in nation-building. That the very farmer was now at the mercy of state atrocities didn't sit well with the people at large.

Critics of the repealed laws point out that one of the reasons for their failure was that the government tried to bulldoze them through without securing the buy-in of stakeholders. It is also noteworthy that while the government had not backed down in the face of protests against some of the contentious decisions that mark its regime—demonetization, abrogation of Article 370 or the citizenship law—the farmers' protest drew retreat.

Second, what made the farmers' protest remarkable is that it weathered several attempts to delegitimize it; the protest took a form whereby it stood above all communities based on religion, class or caste. The anti-nationalist tag did not stick to the protesting farmers—as it has to Muslim-dominant or Opposition party organizations—perhaps because they represent a substantial segment of the Indian economy and compose a variety of religious and cultural groups, including the Hindu Jat community,' writes Jelvin Jose in 'The Farmers' Movement and "Anti-National" Messaging in India'.[6] Clearly, it was difficult to drum up majoritarian sentiments against the farmers' protest. And therein lay its success.

Last but definitely not the least, the entire episode gave the Opposition a new road map on how to counter the 'anti-India' charge that it seemed to constantly be up against.

However, for movements such as the farmers' protest to have a lasting impact and not just a fleeting one, there needs to be what several thinkers have called a shift. These protests, thinkers feel, while being impactful in the moment, struggle to sustain a prolonged influence on electoral politics. To transform sporadic movements like the farmers' protest into enduring political forces, it is felt that several platforms for sustained engagement need to be created. Until these shifts occur, the farmers' protest and similar movements may continue to be fleeting in the larger political landscape of India. Sure enough, during our ground reports from western Uttar Pradesh during the subsequent assembly elections, we found that the farmers' disgruntlement with the government had somewhat ebbed. Speaking to us, Binderpal, a farmer, pointed out how the government had finally been receptive to their demands and had therefore rolled back the laws. His sentiments were echoed by Girija Devi, who believed that farmer interest was foremost in the minds of the BJP.

Come 2024, however, the capital saw Farmers' Protest 2.0, albeit without any trigger this time. Farmers, mostly from Punjab and Haryana, began a renewed push for the Centre to accept their demands, which included legal guarantees for the minimum support price, pensions for farmers and farm labourers and farm debt waiver, implementation of the Swaminathan Commission's recommendations, and more. (The National Commission on Farmers, chaired by Prof. M.S. Swaminathan, submitted five reports from December 2004 to

October 2006. The final report focused on causes of farmer distresses and recommended addressing them through a holistic national policy.)[7]

Unlike the previous protest, which drew support from all sections of society, protest 2.0 has been seen as lacking intensity and displaying overtones of identity politics with two prominent farmer unions spearheading it, while prominent farmer leaders who led the farmers' protest back in 2020–21 have distanced themselves from the stir.

This time the government started the negotiation process even before the farmers' Delhi Chalo march. Despite some progress, including the government agreeing to withdraw cases against protesting farmers, the absence of a legal guarantee for a minimum support price remains a contentious issue. The government has also proposed the formation of a committee to address outstanding concerns. In the meantime, amidst the farm protests, the government has announced a number of measures to empower farmers such as approving the minimum support price for raw jute for 2024–25, a hike in the fair and remunerative price (FRP) for sugar cane by Rs 25 for the 2024–25 season—marking the highest increase since 2014, nutrient-based subsidy rates for the 2024 kharif season and more.

Farm policy experts, in the meantime, argue that one of the main demands of farmers, namely, buying all farm produce at state-set minimum support prices, is economically unviable. On the political front, massive infighting remains the order of the day as the protest is labelled as furthering a politically motivated agenda.

Yet Another Mass Protest

While it is said that it isn't easy to unsettle wrestlers, what with their ability to stay rooted and think on their feet, in January 2023 India's top wrestlers gave up the wrestler's mat and took to the streets in yet another mass protest. The protests were over the lack of action against the head of the country's wrestling federation, Brij Bhushan Sharan Singh, whom they had accused of sexual harassment. The wrestlers, including several Olympic and Asian Games medallists, began a sit-in protest against Singh, which was eventually called off after an assurance that the central government would form a committee to look into the allegations. The protesters resumed their protest in April 2023, citing inaction by authorities and bias by the committee to favour the accused. The wrestlers' protests witnessed high drama when a scuffle broke out between the protesting wrestlers and Delhi Police at the protest site, with the wrestlers claiming that they were manhandled and abused by police personnel. Images of the athletes being dragged away and carried off in buses went viral, sparking criticism. The alleged police crackdown on Olympians went on to create waves of empathy and anger and saw many fence sitters in the public start taking sides. Many saw the treatment meted out to Olympic medal winners as a complete assault on democracy. Delhi Police, however, denied allegations that its officers had assaulted the protesting athletes.

'The way they have made us suffer, I would not want any athlete to win a medal for the country,' wrestler Vinesh Phogat, the first Indian woman wrestler to win a gold at both the Commonwealth and Asian Games, was quoted as saying.[8] Several other wrestlers shared her sentiment. Wrestler Somveer Kadian, who won a bronze medal in the 2018 National Games, questioned the roles of the government, institutions and media during the protest. He lamented that previously, after victories abroad, they were welcomed with flowers and the tricolour upon their return, but during the movement, everything changed suddenly. Expressing his disappointment, he questioned, 'What was wrong in what was being demanded by the wrestlers?'

Another wrestler associated with the movement categorically stated that he did not want to talk about this matter any more as he had distanced himself from the media. Anger was writ large on his face as he recounted facing criticism and even being termed 'anti-national'. He cited an incident where he had once walked 12 kilometres to retrieve a tricolour that had been misplaced whilst he was overseas. He shared how people would stand in respect upon hearing his story; and now those very people were teaching him *'rashtrabhakti'*—love for the nation. The deep disillusionment with the system is also felt in the words of Dr Sunita Godara, a 1992 Asian marathon champion who says that 'the whole ecosystem in sports is rotten where athletes are treated as guinea pigs.'

After the protest site at Jantar Mantar was cleared by the Delhi Police and wrestlers were dragged away and detained, farmers in northern India also decided to stand up for them. The agrarian background of many of the wrestlers had a strong role to play in drawing farmer empathy. Hundreds of farmers and *khap* leaders thronged Delhi's Jantar Mantar, reminding the capital of scenes from the thirteen-month-long farmers' protest. The International Olympic Committee (IOC) and United World Wrestling (UWW) also went on to condemn the police's handling and detention of the Indian wrestlers, calling it 'very disturbing'.

The fact that no FIR was filed by the Delhi Police for a cognizable offence such as sexual harassment until the Supreme Court intervened led opposition parties to allege that the government was shielding Brij Bhushan. Another twist in the tale came when the UWW handed suspension orders to the Wrestling Federation of India (WFI) for not holding presidential elections as scheduled. The WFI elections that followed left the wrestlers further disillusioned as Brij Bhushan took centre stage during the post-victory photo shoot for the newly elected WFI committee where his right-hand man, Sanjay Singh, was elected as the new WFI chief.

In turn, this led to widespread protests, with athletes such as Bajrang Punia leaving his Padma Shri medallion on a footpath in Delhi, while others like Sakshi Malik announced her retirement. The government subsequently suspended the newly elected WFI committee for 'flouting provisions of the National Sports Code' and appearing to be in 'complete control of past office-bearers'. 'The actions smack of complete arbitrariness on the part of the president, which is against the settled principles of good governance and devoid of transparency and due process', the sports ministry noted in its suspension order.[9] After suspending the WFI, the ministry requested the Indian Olympic Association (IOA) to constitute an ad hoc committee to manage and control the affairs of the wrestling federation's governing body.

Athletes like Dr Sunita Godara, however, feel that what has been offered is 'band-aid treatment when surgery is required'. As a long-term solution, she recommends the setting up of a 'proper ethics commission for redressal of grievances'. Sharing her own career story, she states how she began her international career in 1988 with winning an international marathon. 'Each time as per federation rules I had to take permission from the federation to go for international marathons, which was more often than not, denied. I therefore became a rebel. I started going for these marathons on my own and because of that I was not in their good books. This explains why in spite of being shortlisted for the Arjuna Award and Dhyan Chand Award, my name was always shot down. Had there been an ethics panel, I could have gone there and put up my case,' she laments.

What Connects the Wrestlers' Protest to the Farmers' Struggle?

Several parallels have been drawn between the nature of the farmers' and wrestlers' protests and the impact they have had. People who supported the protests feel that both began as peaceful, non-violent demonstrations for justifiable demands. In both cases, while the government initially argued that the protests were limited to protesters from a particular region, they went on to receive mass support from a large cross section of society.

While party leaders defended the government's stance in both these cases, some of them admitted on conditions of anonymity that there seemed to be a perception that the government acts after public pressure begins to mount and that it doesn't show alacrity in quelling protests.

Amidst these high-decibel allegations and counter-allegations, economist Vijay Sardana rings a practical note when he says the learning from both protests is that an effective communication strategy is extremely important. 'Whenever you want to bring a big reform, you should start well in advance by educating people how it is going to impact them. Given the diversity of the country, the government must make use of the powerful electronic media as well as social media to start preparing the society well in advance. They also need to ask people to share their thoughts and actively seek public feedback.' He goes on to sound a note of caution in saying that 'social media has several vested interests who try to create issues irrespective of whoever is in power'. Speaking of the farm laws in particular, he adds that the 'government was a little overconfident that they have a very good law in place. The

Government of India, however, failed in communicating the merits of these laws effectively'.

In sum, the protests, spanning various socio-economic issues like the farmer agitation involving Sikhs from Punjab and Jats from western Uttar Pradesh, cast a shadow over the BJP and the central government in multiple ways. Initially, their direct political impact seemed subdued, but efforts to delegitimize them backfired, revealing unintended consequences. The participation of traditionally BJP-supporting communities in protests against its policies highlighted internal dissent and showcased challenges in maintaining a unified voter base. This discord translated into electoral weakness for the BJP, signalling a shift in public sentiment.

Furthermore, these protests underscored a broader narrative: under BJP governance, grievances of dissenting voices aren't always addressed democratically. This narrative was strategically exploited by opposition parties to criticize the BJP's leadership and policies. Despite these protests not immediately altering electoral outcomes, they significantly influenced public discourse and perception. They also contributed to a narrative where protests served as symbolic resistance against perceived injustices, thereby shaping political discourse and influencing future policy engagements. The participation of diverse communities in these protests also underscored deep-seated grievances and fractured political alignments, posing long-term challenges for the BJP in maintaining its political dominance and managing dissent effectively. These protests therefore have left an indelible mark on Indian politics, resonating beyond immediate electoral gains or losses.

Chapter 3

Balakot Air Strikes;
New Wave of Nationalism

Date: 26 February 2019

Place: Family WhatsApp group comprising three generations

Uncle Balraj: Good evening everyone! What a historic evening.

Uncle Baldev: Absolutely, bhai sahab. It is commendable how India has struck down the biggest training camp of JeM [Jaish-e-Mohammad] in Balakot and killed a large number of terrorists. *Sab theek kehte hain, Modi hai toh mumkin hai*—Modi makes the impossible, possible.

Aunt Santosh: This government is actually committed to taking all necessary measures to fight the menace of terrorism.

Ajay: Aren't we jumping the gun, my dear family? Where is the proof that a large number of JeM terrorists have been killed?

This WhatsApp group is demonstrative of the popular outpourings and messages that were in circulation during these events. The participants in the chat are fictional. Any similarity to actual persons, living or dead, is purely coincidental.

Even India's own statement currently says that since the strike took place only some time ago, they are awaiting details.

Uncle Balraj: What? I can't believe you are saying this. You want proof of the valour of our forces? What has gotten into you young people, that you are doubting your own country?

Uncle Baldev: Really, if this isn't anti-national behaviour, what is?

Vihaan: Ajay Uncle only said that we don't yet know what really happened. How does that qualify as being anti-national? As citizens of India don't we have the right to get some details? It could well be that a strongman image is being projected and national security is being used as a peg ahead of the upcoming elections.

Aunt Santosh: I tell you, this generation is as cynical as it can get. If they can question our armed forces, I don't know what is left. You guys are worse than the Opposition. Or maybe the Opposition is actually working on overdrive to brainwash the young generation.

Ajay: I didn't think a simple comment asking some basic questions could lead to deriding a whole generation. Much as I respect everyone in this group, I am afraid I will not participate in this heightened jingoistic nationalism.

Uncle Balraj: Suits us fine, Ajay. That way we can at least delude ourselves into thinking that no one from our family is against the nation.

Ajay mutes the group.

* * *

India Strikes after Pulwama Terror Attack, Hits Biggest Jaish-e-Mohammed Camp in Balakot[1]

NDTV.com.

26 February 2019

News of India carrying out strikes in Balakot in the Pakistani province of Khyber Pakhtunkhwa, across the Line of Control (LoC), took the entire nation by storm on the evening of 26 February 2019. India's foreign secretary, Vijay Gokhale, issued an official statement confirming that: 'In an intelligence-led operation in the early hours of today, India struck the biggest training camp of JeM [Jaish-e-Mohammed] in Balakot.[2] In this operation, a very large number of JeM terrorists, trainers, senior commanders and groups of jihadis who were being trained for fidayeen action were eliminated.'

The Balakot strike had come in the wake of the 14 February attack on a convoy of vehicles carrying Indian security personnel on the Jammu–Srinagar National Highway connecting Pulwama district with Srinagar in the erstwhile state of Jammu and Kashmir. The attack, one of the deadliest on Indian forces in the region since 1989, had left forty Central Reserve Police Force (CRPF) personnel dead. Subsequently, the militant group Jaish-e-Mohammed, which had emerged as a leading force on the militant landscape, had claimed responsibility for the attack.

While reports on the Balakot strike pegged the number of militants killed at 300, Pakistan was quick to dispute India's death toll estimates, stating that the operation saw Indian jets bomb a hillside without hurting anyone.

Balakot was not the first instance of a premeditated cross-LoC strike being undertaken. In 2016, when terrorists had struck at Poonch and Uri, the response of the Narendra Modi government had been similar, with the army carrying out a surgical strike to wipe out terror launch pads. The strike was supposed to have sent a strong message to Pakistan to think twice before abetting similar operations.

In the days following the Balakot strike, however, with Pakistan launching a counter strike, a thick fog of controversy seemed to be taking over. Was the target of the Indian fighter jets indeed a working camp of the JeM or an abandoned one as claimed by Pakistan? What evidence was there to show that the Indian jets had indeed shot down terrorists and not just a few trees in the vicinity? These and many other such questions were being asked by a section of society. What, according to them, gave their theory credence was the time frame in which these incidents were playing out. The Balakot air strike took place at the end of February in the wake of the Election Commission of India announcing the schedule for the 2019 General Elections. In the days to follow, a purported military operation would also go on to become a political tool, blurring the lines between national security and electoral strategy.

It was pointed out that a few hours after tragedy had struck in Pulwama that took the lives of forty jawans, PM Modi, while addressing a BJP rally in Rudrapur via mobile phone, made no mention of the dastardly attack at Pulwama. While he came under severe attack by the Opposition for his silence on the Pulwama incident, the silence was only short-lived. Come the Balakot strikes, the Pulwama incident found mention in just about every rally. In fact, if prior to Balakot, the government had talked frequently about welfare schemes and economic development, the focus had now shifted to cross-border security. A visit to Ahmedabad saw the PM proclaiming: '*Yeh humara siddhant hai ki hum ghar mein ghus kar maarenge . . . Main lamba intezar nahin kar sakta* (It is our principle to hit the enemy inside its territory . . . I do not like to wait for long).' In a rally in Maharashtra, he made an appeal to first-time voters (treading on shaky ground as per the Election

Commission's Model Code of Conduct, which prohibits political propaganda involving activities of the defence forces) to dedicate their first vote to the Air Force, which had undertaken the air strike at Balakot, and to those jawans who were martyred in Pulwama. In yet another rally in New Delhi, where he spoke in front of a backdrop with the photos of the Indian soldiers who had been killed, his war cry was, 'We won't let this country bow down!' His allies were equally unrestrained in their rallies. At a rally in Patna, Ram Vilas Paswan threw inhibition to the winds by saying, 'Earlier, we used to say that his chest is fifty-six inches. But, today, Gandhi Maidan is honouring you by saying Narendra Modi's chest is not fifty-six inches, but 156 inches.'[3]

It came as no surprise then that the Pulwama and Balakot incidents dominated public opinion. Social media, particularly, was in overdrive when it came to nationalist sentiments. Twitter was soon abuzz with a new hashtag #MainBhiChowkidar, as the PM turned Rahul Gandhi's charge, '*chowkidar chor hai* [the watchman is a thief]', made while raising allegations about irregularities in the Rafale fighter jets deal, into a security issue by projecting himself as the watchman of the nation. As Twitterati took to prefixing chowkidar before his/her name on social media, the chowkidar became a strongman who had avenged the Pulwama killings and was an able defender of the nation.

Recovering the Poll Mojo

Interestingly, with just weeks left for a general election, the Balakot strikes gave the political scenario a strong 'nationalistic' turn. Projected as a decisive response to cross-border terrorism, the strikes established the government's commitment to national security. The narrative had clearly shifted from merely responding to a terrorist attack to showcasing India as an assertive global player. The Balakot strike was also consistently linked to the idea of a 'New India', one that displayed a significant departure from the indecisiveness of the past to an India that was more self-assured.

'The events of Balakot in 2019 became a watershed moment in India's approach towards countering external threats,' says Lieutenant General Sanjay Kulkarni, Ret. DG infantry. 'Before Balakot, India's responses to provocations from across the border were tempered with caution and a deliberate stance. However, the strike on Balakot showcased a paradigm shift in India's strategy, indicating a clear message that transgressions against the nation's security wouldn't go unanswered,' he adds. He gives several examples to substantiate his point. 'In 2001, during the Parliament attack, India did not take any action. There was indeed deliberation. Even after the 2008 Mumbai attacks, we didn't fully teach Pakistan a lesson. Again, there was deliberation. However, in 2019, the scenario changed, and during Balakot, we sent a message that such actions won't be tolerated any more.' He recalls how 'there used to be a saying at the border that the Pakistani army would tell the Indian army, "Our authority is in our hands, while yours comes from Delhi." This mindset has now changed. The army is no longer hesitant to move from authority to action. It's not necessary to resort to gunfire every time, but it has instilled confidence.'

Consequently, what the Balakot episode did was not only showcase the military prowess of the nation, but also shape its political landscape. As nationalistic fervour gripped the nation, the ruling BJP was also quick to zero in on the catchy slogan of 'Modi *hai to mumkin hai*, Modi makes the impossible, possible', projecting the PM as the guardian of India's security interests, leveraging the sentiment of national pride to consolidate its support base.

While political figures using the spirit of nationalism to drive votes isn't new, this time was different. Political commentator and columnist Asim points out the difference between 'the nationalism of Indira Gandhi and the present Modi phase', for instance. 'The nationalism of Indira Gandhi merely underlined the principle that Congress alone represented the national interests while others merely represented sectional interests. Additionally, the formulation of the national interest in the case of Indira Gandhi's nationalism was vague. It was untethered to any stable intellectual or political foundation. Thus, it could be credibly challenged. The present BJP's nationalism is grounded in its long-standing ideology of Hindutva, which provides an independent foundation of legitimacy. Second, charismatic leadership in the Indian context is often based on a certain notion of selfless/desire-less political action on behalf of the nation. Modi and Yogi can draw on this model better than Indira Gandhi could, as her personality could not be separated from her attachment to children (and consequent need for material acquisitiveness).'

Whatever the reasons, the transformation of the Balakot strike into a symbol of national strength resonated with a significant section of the electorate. What was shifting along the way, therefore, were poll trends.

As a part of our on-the-ground coverage in Odisha in April 2019, we witnessed these trends first-hand. Here was a state that was witnessing simultaneous assembly and Lok Sabha polls. While Naveen Patnaik continued to be a popular chief minister, Prime Minister Narendra Modi had placed himself firmly in Odisha's backyard as the BJP was positioning itself as the opposition party in the state dominated by the Biju Janta Dal. At Ravenshaw University in Cuttack, one of India's oldest universities, we heard a group of students talk about the achievements of New India, a strong election plank of the BJP.

That the 2016 Uri surgical strikes and the 2019 Balakot air strikes showcased the diplomatic achievements of India seemed to be a common belief. The feeling of nationalism was so dominant that young first-time voters saw PM Modi as 'a hero who could do the unthinkable—a man who always believes in holding the India flag high'. Rajni, a first-time voter, in fact pointed out that 'India today wouldn't settle for less as PM Modi was there to protect Indians.' Even dynasty—another issue raised by the BJP—found resonance with a student in the group claiming, '*Na parivaarvad, na jaatiwad sabse pehle rashtravaad* (nationalism before nepotism).'

If Odisha, which had so far been untouched by nationalism, was witnessing its waves post the Balakot strikes, Uttar Pradesh was thriving on it. Close to a rally ground in Hamirpur district in Uttar Pradesh, we met nineteen-year-old Rajiv Kumar who was intently watching something on his mobile phone while Mayawati's rally was in progress. Kumar confessed he was listening to one of PM Modi's speeches—'*Inse koi dushman bach nahin sakta, sabko aukaat dikhate hain* (he can show India's enemies their true place).' A first-time voter, he wasn't unduly worried about his own future or the job market. '*Agar desh mazboot hoga to sab achcha hoga, padhayi, naukri sab milegi* (If the nation is secure, development will follow),' he said with unflinching passion.

It is interesting to note that the wave of nationalism took root not just in India, but also among the Indian diaspora, who were equally vocal in their support for a strong stance on national security. 'As an Indian-Australian, I keenly observed the aftermath of the Balakot air strikes and its influence on Indian politics. The pride and fervour that swept through the Indian diaspora, including here in Australia, was palpable. It reflected a deep-seated commitment to national security and a sense of solidarity with the motherland,' recounts Akashika Mohla, an Australia-based media, policy, advocacy and international affairs expert. She further elaborates on the phenomenon by adding a historical perspective. 'My uncle, a war veteran, rightly pointed out that throughout history, India has been a victim of terrorism from its aggressive neighbours, be it in 1971 during former PM Indira Gandhi's regime with the Bangladesh Liberation war or during PM Narendra Modi's regime—the Pulwama attacks in 2019. Both leaders, in their times, had landslide victories following public support for their strong, decisive and determined leadership during periods of crisis. The political acumen to effectively leverage national sentiment in support of war or attack is perhaps the talisman behind the political win, despite Marxist versus nationalist values.'

Rahul Verma, Fellow, Centre for Policy Research (CPR), brings in yet another perspective when he adds to the discussion the advantage that incumbent governments have. 'While we do not have hard evidence to measure the extent to which nationalistic sentiments play on the mind of Indian voters, we know that incumbent governments in general, and much more in the case of a right-wing incumbent, have an advantage at the time of a national security crisis,' he opines. 'Let me just elaborate on this with what we have seen across the globe. Whenever there is a national security crisis, we find a rallying around the flag effect. This is the term that has been used especially in the American context, implying that in a situation of national security, crisis or war, the popularity of incumbent leaders increases, while economic concerns related to the performance of the economy and performance of the government decrease. In this sense they are far more likely to reap the benefits of a national security crisis. In the Indian case, if you think of 2019, there is an emerging consensus that the terror attack in Pulwama and India's response of conducting a strike across the LoC created a kind of rally around the flag

effect. This is not to say that had the Pulwama–Balakot event
not happened, the BJP would not have become the single largest
party or would not have been close to winning the election, but
this event created a favourable environment for them.'

Coming back to the situation on the ground, what was
growing beyond bounds was the confidence of the ruling party.
B.S. Yediyurappa, the BJP leader of Karnataka, even predicted
that the air strike had created a mood in favour of Prime
Minister Modi and would help the BJP win twenty-two of
the twenty-eight Lok Sabha seats in Karnataka. When visuals
of the capture of Wing Commander Abhinandan Varthaman
and his eventual release by the Pakistan military hit the media,
Pakistan, Pulwama, Balakot and terrorism undisputedly became
the central issues of the Lok Sabha elections. In the final
analysis, it was the 'nationalist sentiment' around security that
helped BJP hit the home run in the 2019 Lok Sabha election.

No Room for Dissent

It stood to reason that the rhetoric that portrayed the Balakot
strikes as an act of supreme nationalism also, by contrast,
portrayed any criticism of it as an attack on the armed forces
and by extension, an attack on the nation itself.

The Opposition took to pointing out how the episode
effectively stifled dissent and limited the scope to question
the government's actions without risking accusations of being
'anti-national'. When Sam Pitroda, close confidant of Rahul
Gandhi and chairman of the Overseas Indian National
Congress, said in an interview to ANI, 'I would like to
know more as I have read in the *New York Times* and other
newspapers, what did we really attack, we really killed 300
people?',[4] PM Modi hit out at the Opposition in a series of
tweets alleging it had insulted the armed forces. 'Is this the way

you are serving the national interest? You may question me on my policies. You may not trust me but at least trust the armed forces. Don't raise questions over their valour,' PM Modi said just days after the airstrike.[5] Amidst the clamour for 'proof' of damage to Pakistani terror installations by several opposition leaders including Mamta Banerjee and Mehbooba Mufti, the decibel level of pronouncing them 'anti-national' as also 'terror apologists and questioners of our armed forces', was far higher.

Congress member of Parliament (MP) Shashi Tharoor while speaking at the India Today Conclave, summed up the Opposition's conundrum: 'The Opposition was in a bind. To question whose fault it was that forty coffins went back to villages in India, whose security lapses resulted in these forty deaths, would have been seen somehow as unpatriotic.' He further added, 'It would have been unpatriotic to say whether your (government's) Balakot bombings took out any terrorists or did you hit a bunch of trees on a deserted hillside as the international media is claiming . . . tell us what the proof is. We didn't say it because we felt we have to stand by the soldiers . . . we have to be with the flag . . . with the air force. As a result, we denied ourselves a legitimate critique of the national security, posturing which the government ran away with northern India,' Tharoor concluded.[6]

Congress leaders also admitted that in the light of the new nationalism wave they needed to recalibrate their strategy and take a fresh look at things. Forced on to the back foot, opposition parties were struggling to bring economic issues back into focus as also to find a viable way to deny BJP the glory of the cross-LoC strike.

Political observers point out that the Balakot air strikes were not the first time during the Modi government's tenure that the BJP had tried to shift the public discourse towards nationalism. 'Since 2014, the BJP has left no stone unturned to make nationalism a salient issue. In 2016, after pro-separatist slogans were raised at Delhi's Jawaharlal Nehru University, the BJP was quick to react and use it as an opportunity to attack its opponents for being too soft on separatism and accused them of being "anti-national",' Pranav Gupta and Dishil Shrimankar point out in their article titled 'How Nationalism Helped the BJP'.[7] Speaking of the difference in the impact of recent happenings in Indian electoral politics, namely the farmers' protest and the Balakot air strikes, experts also point out that the farmers' protest could not create a lasting influence on Indian electoral politics, perhaps because the farmers were not a separate political class in India. The Balakot air strike, on the other hand, was pertinent in creating nationalist sentiment, which played an important role in the 2019 General Elections.

In ground reports it was found that several farmers from Maharashtra, for instance, who had voted for the Hindu nationalist BJP in the 2014 general election, had made up their minds to vote for the opposition Congress in 2019. The air strikes, however, changed all of that. PM Modi was seen as 'teaching a lesson to Pakistan' and therefore deserved their vote. Before the 2019 General Elections, as a part of our extensive on-the-ground reportage when we were passing through the villages of Bayasi in Purnia, Bihar, we happened to meet a group of villagers. Among them was Mahavir Paswan, a thirty-five-year-old. When our conversation veered towards who he would vote for in the forthcoming elections, he replied with an unequivocal 'Modi', claiming that Modi had entered 'Pakistan's house and attacked them'. During further conversation, Paswan confirmed that discussions in their village mostly revolved around the Balakot air strike and that while several of them were unhappy with Modi since demonetization, the air strike had changed their opinion. 'Only when the country is secure will things be set right,' he pointed out with a sense of finality.

Not everyone looked at the Balakot strike with the same black-and-white lens, though. Author and former diplomat Pavan Varma in an op-ed in *Times of India* added nuance to this view and detailed how in the current times, 'patriotism is considered somewhat inferior unless it manifests itself in its hyper version of overt nationalism.' He went on to add that 'National security is a bipartisan priority. The armed forces are mandated to be apolitical. Their valour and sacrifice is not the monopoly of any one party. To make them an accessory to party politics may help to stoke nationalism but is an unpatriotic act. For the government to take due credit for taking decisive action is legitimate; to co-opt this process, the armed forces is not.'[8]

Whether or not we agree with his views, one thing is clear. With the Indian Air Force air strike against the Balakot terrorist camp in Pakistan, the BJP had scored a significant political victory. The war cry for the 2019 General Elections was sounded with nationalism and national security being key electoral issues. There was also no doubt that among the Balakot casualties, at least in the immediate term, was the Opposition, which was left bereft of any matching rhetoric. As for the politics of 'nationalism', it was here to stay.

Post 2019, however, the theme of nationalism underwent some changes. Particularly when it came to the opposition parties, they not only corrected their course on this issue but also formulated their own definition of nationalism. Whether it was issues concerning the youth, farmers or other related matters, everything was linked to nationalism. In an interview on the question of how to counter strong nationalism, Priyanka Gandhi told me that patriotism isn't limited to simply loving the country; it also entails loving its people. It involves fighting for their interests and rights. Following the lessons of 2019, all opposition parties began countering BJP's brand of nationalism in every protest, demonstration and rally they held. Their own rallies began featuring the national flag. Meanwhile, the BJP also softened its stance on this issue.

Somewhere, the impact of all this was evident in the results of the 2024 General Elections. Experts have argued that the BJP's linking of every minor issue with nationalism and associating opponents with anti-national sentiments began to disconnect the common people. This trend extended to matters of religion as well. Even senior party leaders, including Uma Bharti, one of the most prominent names associated with the Ram Temple movement, cautioned the BJP after its defeat in Ayodhya, saying, 'You must understand the pulse of the Hindu society. Not every Ram devotee will vote for BJP. We should not harbor the arrogance that those who do not vote for us are not Ram devotees.'[9] Clearly this sentiment also applied to nationalism.

In fact, BJP's strategy of integrating nationalism into various aspects of governance and public discourse has had profound implications. It has polarized public opinion, with supporters viewing the party as the sole custodian of national interests and opponents being branded as unpatriotic. This narrative, however, risks alienating sections of society who do not align with the BJP's version of nationalism. Uma Bharti's critique underscores a broader concern that excessive nationalism might be driving a wedge between the party and its traditional supporters.

Moreover, tying every political debate to nationalism can oversimplify complex issues and stifle genuine dialogue. While national pride is important, critics argue that it should not overshadow other pressing concerns such as economic development, social welfare and inclusive governance. Therefore, while nationalism can be a unifying force, its instrumentalization in political rhetoric requires careful consideration to avoid marginalizing diverse voices within the nation.

While BJP's approach to nationalism reflects a broader global trend where political parties harness identity politics to consolidate power, it also poses challenges in maintaining social cohesion and inclusive governance.

Chapter 4

When a Deadly Virus Meets Viral Nationalism

Time: Sometime in April 2020, amidst the raging Covid-19 pandemic.

Place: Yet another family WhatsApp group

Aunt Sarla: Just what are these Corona Bombs up to? Here we are cut off from the world outside, biding a difficult time and they have the audacity to hold these meetings and kill us all.

Uncle Yash: Really behenji. They have taken Corona Jihad to another level. And now they are refusing to go into quarantine, assaulting hospital staff and what not. I mean these super spreaders deserve to die themselves, not kill all of us.

Uncle Rakesh: I hope you all saw the video that showed these Muslims intentionally sneezing on each other to spread the virus. I am appalled.

This WhatsApp group is demonstrative of the popular outpourings and messages that were in circulation during these events. The participants in the chat are fictional. Any similarity to actual persons, living or dead, is purely coincidental.

Kavya: Wasn't that video called out as being fake? I think there is a lot of misinformation doing the rounds as well. We need to be careful with it, as much as we are with the virus.

Niyati: I agree. I mean, we seem to be hitting out at a whole community; there are videos doing the rounds asking people not to buy from Muslim shops. This is Islamophobia taken to a whole new level.

Aunt Sarla: You youngsters are very naive. Much as you want to believe in the goodness of all, remember that there are lives at stake. I hope you girls have heard of bioweapons. This is exactly what we are witnessing now.

Uncle Yash: True.

Kavya (private message to Niyati): I give up! It is pointless to explain to them that these are fake videos.

* * *

India Under Lockdown

'In order to protect the country, and each of its citizens, from midnight tonight, a full ban is being imposed on people from stepping out of their homes. All the states in the country, all the union territories, each district, each municipality, each village, each locality is being put under lockdown . . . This is a necessary step in the decisive fight against corona pandemic . . . Considering the circumstances at present, this lockdown will last twenty-one days. The next twenty-one days are of critical importance for us.' PM Modi in his address to the nation in March 2020.[1]

When the world had celebrated the dawn of a new decade with the usual revelry just a few months prior, few could have imagined what 2020 had in store. Nobody knew then that the novel coronavirus was waiting to wreak havoc, that it would devastate communities and bring the world economy to its knees. The heartbreak of loved ones dying alone in hospitals, with even bedside visits considered too dangerous to risk, was to be the destiny of many.

The crisis couldn't have come at a worse time for India. The country was already in tumult over the CAA which offered amnesty to non-Muslim immigrants from Pakistan, Bangladesh and Afghanistan. It was believed that the CAA was introducing for the first time in independent India's history, a religious test for citizenship. Shaheen Bagh and its protesters were making international headlines, with women taking to the streets to protest against the Act peacefully, persistently. Just a month earlier, in February of 2020, the national capital of Delhi had seen the deepening of the sectarian divide and exacerbated religious tensions leading to communal riots.

To his credit, PM Modi, unlike several Western leaders, did not try to downplay the potential impact of the virus, offering instead a robust response to curb the spread of infections. After the death toll from the virus crossed twelve, a twenty-one-day stringent lockdown was declared for the entire country. This move, while necessary for public health, did not come without its challenges. The sudden halt in economic activities brought about immense hardships for many. For India's estimated 120 million migrant labourers, particularly, the lockdown turned out to be a bigger crisis as wages dried up and many could not afford rent or even food in the cities. What followed was the spectre of the long walk home of India's migrant workers, lugging their life's belongings, oftentimes with infants in tow; an event that is likely to weigh heavily on the nation's collective consciousness for times to come. The plight of the migrant workers underscored a critical failure in governmental planning and response. The scenes of labourers walking hundreds of kilometres, often without adequate food or shelter, highlighted a disconnect between policy decisions and ground realities. This failure was not just logistical but also humanitarian.

As the crisis unfolded further, India focused on relief measures as also on developing its own capabilities in manufacturing essential medical supplies, laying the groundwork for a more self-sufficient and resilient healthcare infrastructure. In response to the death and chaos caused by the coronavirus, India's scientific community worked tirelessly to develop and manufacture indigenous vaccines.

Says Dr Randeep Guleria, pulmonologist and the ex-director of the All India Institute of Medical Sciences (AIIMS), 'The Covid crisis showed that India is a resilient nation. During this period, we did a lot of work to convert, restructure and prepare infrastructure to handle patients. It was a roller-coaster ride but as compared to a lot of Western countries, we were able to do a good job. There was an unprecedented display of national unity and individual responsibility to save the country. The most significant impact was that people listened, whether it was about political leadership or medical science.' Speaking about the initial hurdles, he goes on to add that 'there was chaos and panic initially, people were apprehensive, and everything seemed tangled. Various misconceptions on social media complicated matters. Establishing Covid centres, implementing lockdowns, or managing the supply chain posed challenges everywhere in the country. It was believed that India wouldn't be able to manage Covid due to its population and infrastructure limitations, especially in reaching remote villages. However, through mass movement, we proved it wrong. Challenges came and were overcome. Somewhere within the country, the sense of nationalism played a significant role. People showed that they had to save not only themselves but also the country and society. Responsibility was taken voluntarily. This unprecedented factor led to our success.' Speaking of the vaccine in particular, he adds how it wasn't believed that 'people would willingly take the Covid vaccine in such large numbers. Yet, people not only took it themselves but also encouraged others. While developed countries faced resistance, we emerged as leaders in vaccine distribution. This is not to deny that issues based on religion created difficulties during Covid. Whether it was about the content of the Covid vaccine or implications for gender, challenges arose. Yet, people themselves dismissed these issues. Especially enlightened individuals stepping forward to get vaccinated eliminated barriers. Soon, we became one of the countries giving the most Covid vaccines. India's biggest advantage was that resistance to such issues came from a small section, and the larger populace stood together in the fight. Whereas, in other countries, both sections were equally strong.'

Priyam Gandhi-Mody, in her book *A Nation to Protect: Leading India through the Covid Crisis*, echoes similar sentiments and has described how India battled and emerged from the deadly crisis under the leadership of Prime Minister Narendra Modi. She points out that Prime Minister Modi's robust grip on the administration changed India's fortunes in the fight against the virus as he took absolute control of the country's response mechanisms and streamlined systems to cut red tape. She points out that the country has proved the cynics wrong with one of the lowest fatality rates.[2]

Critics, however, point out that that these claims not withstanding, India experienced a severe downturn exacerbated by the Covid-19 pandemic. The disruption caused by the lockdowns had a ripple effect across various sectors, leading to job losses, reduced consumer spending and a contraction in

GDP growth. The government's initial efforts to contain the virus and support the economy were lauded during the first wave. However, as the second wave struck with unprecedented ferocity, the response appeared reactive and insufficient. Critical shortages of medical supplies, overwhelmed healthcare facilities and a surge in fatalities marked this period, further denting public confidence in the administration's ability to manage the crisis effectively.

Prime Minister Narendra Modi, who had previously enjoyed widespread popularity, faced intense scrutiny and criticism during this tumultuous period. The perception of a delayed and inadequate response to the second wave tarnished his image and tested the resilience of his leadership. Public trust, once a cornerstone of his political capital, wavered amidst widespread suffering and hardship.

In retrospect, the Covid-19 pandemic laid bare systemic vulnerabilities in India's governance and healthcare infrastructure. The lessons learnt from this crisis underscored the urgent need for robust, proactive measures to address future health emergencies and economic shocks effectively. As the country strives to recover and rebuild, the scars of this challenging period serve as a poignant reminder of the importance of foresight, transparency and inclusive policies in safeguarding public welfare and national resilience.

Viral Nationalism

While the pandemic soared, and along with it relief measures were stepped up, a phenomenon that saw an upward trajectory was the rise of 'viral nationalism'. Right at the beginning of the pandemic, PM Modi had called for nationwide solidarity, asking the people of the country to demonstrate their appreciation for Indian doctors and health workers. The prime minister's call resonated with millions as the sound of the banging of plates, blowing of conch shells and bursting of crackers reverberated in the air as the clock struck five on 22 March. Besides expressing gratitude to those providing essential services, the event also acquired a pseudoscientific colour with several people, including megastar Amitabh Bachchan, claiming that the vibrations from clapping and blowing conch shells would have reduced or destroyed the potency of the coronavirus as it was 'amavasya', the darkest day of the month. Soon, family WhatsApp groups were buzzing with messages to say that the applause Prime Minister Narendra Modi had organized for health workers had been detected by a 'bio-satellite' that confirmed the weakening of the virus. Other theories claiming to fight the novel virus such as 'if we do yoga, mud bath and blow conch shells, no Covid will touch us'[3] also trickled in from several other quarters, including from lawmakers. The 'coronavirus infodemic' was clearly not just as potent as the pandemic, it was also poised to take a menacing turn.

Us vs Them

At the centre of the controversy that turned the war from being 'us versus the virus' to becoming 'us versus them' was a Muslim missionary movement—the Tablighi Jamaat. An international gathering of Tablighis—preachers or a society to spread the faith—had taken place in New Delhi's Nizamuddin area in March 2020, drawing hundreds of foreign nationals from countries such as Thailand, Nepal, Myanmar, Indonesia, Bangladesh, Malaysia, Sri Lanka and Kyrgyzstan. Despite a government order prohibiting large gatherings, more than 4500 people had assembled at the headquarters of the Tablighi Jamaat. In any country where the pandemic was fast claiming lives, a gathering of this scale was certainly a horrific display of irresponsibility and an area of legitimate concern. That it should stoke a wave of sectarian, toxic nationalism, injecting religion into a pandemic and a communal colour to the fight against it, however, seemed far-fetched. Yet it was this event that went on to put India at the top of Covid-related hostilities against certain religious groups, as per a report by the Pew Research Centre, a Washington-based think tank.[4]

On 22 March when authorities shut the doors of the five-storey headquarters of the Tablighi Jamaat with about 2500 worshippers still inside, the large-scale rhetoric that followed painted an entire community as a vector of disease and an insidious threat. As hashtags such as #CoronaJihad and #TablighiVirus trended on social media, the idea of the Muslim as the 'threatening other' also became fodder for several television stations who left no stones unturned in referring to it as a 'deliberate' and 'callous' conspiracy, further unleashing divisiveness. As opposed to reporting the catastrophic lapse on the part of both the Jamaat and the state authorities, the media seemed to be focused on unleashing a propaganda war with its inflammatory invective.

Not only did both the Union and the Delhi governments keep marking the *markaz* as the centre of this 'anti-national conspiracy' of 'Corona Jihad', the relentless media attention on the event also made its way into the health ministry's daily press briefing, where the number of cases linked to the incident were separately reported.

By early April, some television channels had begun to insist that over 30 per cent of the corona-positive cases had the 'Tablighi Virus' based on reports from the ministry of family health and welfare.[5]

What this led to, were reports of Muslims facing discrimination, violence as well as attacks by vigilante groups.[6] As misinformation was rife, there were reports of vegetable vendors from the community being stopped from selling vegetables, accused of being members of the Tablighi Jamaat and spreading the coronavirus. A video showing Muslims intentionally sneezing on each other to spread the virus did the rounds before it was called out as being fake.[7] Though quickly debunked, the rumours of Tablighi Jamaat members refusing to go into quarantine, assaulting hospital staff and throwing bottles of urine at Hindus also quickly spread. As reports of people from the markaz travelling to different parts of India poured in, the hate became even more vicious. 'The heightened media coverage of the event had serious ramifications for intercommunal relations in India and could result in increased prejudices against India's largest minorities. Fake news and videos happened to be the most important vehicles of the spread of hate,' Parth Sharma and Abhijit Anand noted in Indian media coverage of the Nizamuddin markaz event during the Covid-19 pandemic.[8] It was almost as if the country at large had needed someone to blame for the misery of their Covid devastated lives.

'The behaviour of some members of a sect is being read as a predilection of *all* Muslims. Muslims crowd together in ghettos; Muslims are irrationally religious; Muslims want to spread the disease and harm Hindus . . . The "imagined Muslim" is seen as an untrustworthy foreign element in the Hindu body politic that needs to be expunged, the way a dangerous virus is fought against,' opines Professor Dibyesh Anand, author of *Hindu Nationalism in India and the Politics of Fear.*[9]

Even when several Muslims came out publicly to condemn the action of the Jamaat and Muslim clergy, and intellectuals from the community also issued an appeal to the government that it wasn't the time to find fault and that any attempt to give the event 'a sectarian twist would weaken our battle against the deadly virus',[10] the polarized discourse continued to look at an entire community to be in the wrong and labelled them as 'superspreaders'. Amidst the worsening invective, there finally came a tweet from the Prime Minister's Office to say that 'Covid-19 does not see race, religion, colour, cast, creed, language or borders before striking. Our response and conduct therefore should attach primacy to unity and brotherhood.'[11] The harm, however, was already done. To borrow the words of a social media user, the plague of communal hatred had made Covid-19 seem like a common cold. It was almost as if Covid-19 had miraculously acquired a religion.

Not everyone, however, saw it this way. 'Communalism hasn't come suddenly only because you have a BJP government,' opines Zafar Sareshwala, an Ahmedabad-based businessman and a confidant of Modi. 'I am from Ahmedabad, Gujarat, and Gujarat has been the epicentre of riots. I remember very vividly as I was five years old when the 1969 riots happened. That was the worst in Indian history after Independence, more than 5000 people were killed in Ahmedabad city alone. When the 1981 riots happened, I was in class twelve. It started as an anti-reservation movement but was given a communal colour. Between 1985 and 1987, there used to be riots every three/four months. After that I witnessed the riot of 1990 post Advani's rath yatra. These were followed by the 1992 riots post Babri Masjid, and then 2002 riots. I remember witnessing calls such as "*musalman ka bahishkar karo*"—ban Muslims—after every riot. At the time people used to distribute *patrikas* and put it on billboards. There were even calls like don't buy from Bata as they thought it was a Muslim company. Only in those days there was no social media that multiplied everything manifold,' he adds. Sareshwala goes on to reason that calls of banning Muslim vendors have little meaning—'These calls aren't new and don't have much impact. If I am *imaandar and amanatdar* (honest and trustworthy), who won't buy from a store of such a shopkeeper?' he asks. As an example, he recounts an incident where he was conducting a programme in Ranchi a couple of years ago. 'That year, incidentally, the toppers of the tenth and twelfth board exams were both Muslim girls, so we were rewarding them. In the papers that day there was news that Praveen Togadia (doctor, advocate for Hindu Nationalism) and Ashok Singhal (former president of Vishwa Hindu Parishad) had taken a stopover at Ranchi as their helicopters had developed a technical snag. I asked the people in the gathering to tell me [that] if there [were] two helicopter mechanics—Abdur Rehman who had repaired 5000 helicopters in the past and Gangaram who had repaired only 700 helicopters—whom would they ask for help? The answer was obvious. Whipping up passion alone doesn't work, it has to be backed by several other things,' he says with seemingly relentless logic.

Speaking of facts, it deserves a mention here that in the months to follow, forty-four accused who were charged with contravening emergency rules by participating in the Jamaat congregation were later exonerated by a metropolitan court. The court's observations: 'None of them were present at the markaz on the relevant period and they had been picked up from different places so as to maliciously prosecute them upon directions from the Ministry of Home Affairs,'[12] spoke volumes about the country's worsening communal narrative. The Aurangabad bench of the Bombay High Court also criticized the 'scapegoating' of Tablighis for the pandemic. 'It is now time to "repent this action" and take positive steps to "repair the damage,"[13] it said. As for the Nizamuddin markaz, it was initially opened through an interim order of the Delhi High Court for the offering of namaz under the strict surveillance of CCTV cameras. The keys of the mosque were handed over for complete reopening much later, once again, after the Delhi High Court's intervention.

Amidst the propaganda war that only deepened pre-existing communal fault lines, what is also important to dwell upon is what political analyst Rahul Verma calls the 'complex interplay between crises, political outcomes, and public perception'. He points out how the 'Covid-19 pandemic reshaped political landscapes worldwide. For instance, the United States 2020 election witnessed former President Trump's loss amidst the crisis. This exemplifies how a crisis can affect electoral outcomes. In India, Prime Minister Modi effectively utilized the crisis to evoke nationalist sentiments, showcasing the potential for leaders to leverage crises for political gains.'

Similar sentiments are echoed by senior JDU leader K.C. Tyagi, who feels that while 'any government had very limited options in the face of the pandemic, during this time all governments also utilized the opportunity to enhance their political power and outreach to the public'. He goes on to add that '[I]t's an established fact that during any major crisis, nationalism emerges as the strongest narrative in society. The same happened during Covid. Nationalistic sentiments prevailed not only in India but also in other countries. We witnessed the effects even in the form of reverse globalization and reverse migration. When millions of labourers returned to their homes, it became a significant political issue. Nitish Kumar, (chief minister of Bihar) for instance, benefited politically from his management of the labour situation during the assembly elections. He returned to power. Similarly, Narendra Modi's initiation of free ration during this period became his strongest support base. People felt the need for a strong and decisive government to tackle the crisis. Modi also gained politically from this.' In sum, Tyagi feels that 'Covid became a crucial means to strengthen the nationalist phase in the country and globally'. He, however, also goes on to sound a note of caution when he says that 'it is also suggested that aggressive nationalism will rise globally, making free trade difficult. Leaders who govern arbitrarily might exploit the benefits of the pandemic, strengthening themselves while imposing various restrictions and surveillance on the public.'

It is true that Covid-19 significantly altered the direction of governance in India. During Covid-19, the concept of self-reliance and the nationalism that it spawned may not have persisted for long, but its side effects were visible far and wide. The central government's initiation of the free ration scheme marked the beginning of a new political strategy. Initially introduced as temporary relief for the economically vulnerable affected by Covid-19, the scheme continued even after the pandemic due to its popularity and the political dividends it yielded. In various opinion polls, the government's free ration scheme was deemed the most significant voter-catching initiative. Opposition parties launched counter schemes such as offering fixed wages to women to negate its impact, which also garnered support. Later, the central government extended the free ration scheme until 2029. According to analysts, now no government can afford to ignore this scheme.

In fact, the new plan of benevolent statesmanship linked with nationalism has now become an inevitable part of politics.

Whether or not we agree with this political analysis, what is clear is that while the virus tested the robustness and contingencies of the country's healthcare systems, the fear of the virus also went on to amplify existing prejudices at a time when the nation needed to fight a common enemy. Amidst Covid-19 crippling nearly every aspect of life in India, if there was one department that was thriving, it was the department of hate and fake news that was fuelled by the Indian cyber hate machine and the airwaves.

Chapter 5

Nationalism Goes Global

Time: September 2019

Place: WhatsApp group of Indian immigrants in the US

Ashok: Who all am I seeing at the Howdy Modi event? I believe this is an event that will take bilateral ties to a new level.

Sunil: You bet! Trump and Modi addressing 50,000 Indian Americans in Houston is big for the diaspora all right, but also for both the countries.

Reena: I couldn't agree more. I don't think President Trump has shared a dais with a visiting foreign leader like this before. Tell me, are you all planning to be dressed in ethnic finery?

Manisha: Of course.

Ashok: Wear what you will, as long as you wear the love for Modi on your sleeve. The guy is a game changer.

This WhatsApp group is demonstrative of the popular outpourings and messages that were in circulation during these events. The participants in the chat are fictional. Any similarity to actual persons, living or dead, is purely coincidental.

Saisha: Sorry about being the party pooper, but I really think everything is being blown out of proportion, what with these WhatsApp forwards and overt nationalist messaging. The new generation, of course, is being presented these messages by way of a brand new Instagram packaging. Amidst all the hoopla, you all surely know of the protests that are being organized on the sidelines of the event around the caste-based violence in India?

Sunil: I don't think a historic occasion such as this one should be marred by people who have little understanding of the change Modi is driving. He has done so much to bring India on to the world stage. I think the cynics need to take a chill pill!

Saisha: There you go! Yet another place where dissent is forbidden!

* * *

Diaspora Diplomacy

When India's Prime Minister Narendra Modi and the US President Donald Trump raised their clasped hands on stage at the blockbuster Howdy Modi event in Houston, Texas, in 2019, more than 50,000 people burst into loud applause. The two leaders had earlier made a grand entrance to the beats of bhangra drummers filling the NRG Stadium, one of Houston's largest football stadiums, as chants of 'Modi' and 'USA' reverberated in the air. This was a spectacle that the US had witnessed before. Earlier, in 2014, when PM Modi had visited the storied Madison Square Garden in New York City, the place was abuzz with 20,000 people, many of whom had painted his face on their person.

Come to think of it, engagement with overseas Indian communities at this scale may seem odd, given that political parties have to win elections on the back of the electorate back home and that India as a country does not allow non-resident Indians (NRIs) to cast ballots remotely. In fact, up until 2010, NRIs were not allowed to vote in the elections at all. An amendment in 2011 granted them the right to vote at their particular constituency in India provided they had not acquired citizenship of any other country. The voting, however, requires their physical presence at the particular polling booth, making the process nearly unviable. The Representation of the People (Amendment) Bill, 2017, subsequently proposed to extend proxy voting rights to overseas Indians. The bill, however, lapsed with the dissolution of the sixteenth Lok Sabha. The Election Commission's proposal for introducing electronically transmitted postal ballots is currently pending with the government.

That said, the diaspora of an estimated 32 million Indians and people of Indian origin—spread across the globe—is an important resource for any political party in India. Not only is India one of the world's biggest recipients of foreign remittances (India received close to $90 billion in remittance flows from around the world in 2021–22, the highest received in a single year), in terms of political influence too, NRIs are known to aggressively campaign for elections back home.

What works particularly well for the ruling BJP is what a number of academics and observers of the diaspora have pointed out—the traditional voter base of the BJP tends to find a reflection in the demographic make-up of the diaspora.

The Indian diaspora, of course, is not a recent phenomenon. But for a long time, they were cut off from mainland India in many ways. The only sign of nationalism they expressed was perhaps during cricket matches with India in the running. A part of this disconnection can be traced back to India's traditional stance of largely disengaging with the diaspora. At the time of India's founding, Jawaharlal Nehru adopted a policy of 'active disassociation' from the diaspora, choosing not to intervene in another country's sovereignty, writes Sreeram Chaulia, a professor at India's Jindal School of International Affairs and author of *Modi Doctrine, The Foreign Policy of India's Prime Minister*. In the '70s and '80s, NRIs were even branded as 'non-responsible Indians' or the perhaps worse 'non-reliable Indians'; the thought process being that they had succumbed to widespread 'brain drain' and deserted the motherland for greener pastures. Their patriotism was therefore always circumspect. It was only the era of globalization and privatization in the 1990s under then prime minister Rajiv Gandhi that saw an increased involvement of the diaspora. The Congress Party did not, however, witness a major influence among the diaspora, except perhaps in the Gulf countries, the construct of whose NRI populace reflected in their vote bank. The Overseas Friends of the BJP (OFBJP), on the other hand, was formed as early as 1992 and has since mobilized support and campaigned for the party at large. In 2003, the BJP under then prime minister Atal Bihari Vajpayee even went on to launch the Pravasi Bharatiya Divas, or the Indian diaspora day, to celebrate the successes of Indians abroad. That said, the scale of the 'diaspora diplomacy' deployed by PM Modi to recruit India's overseas community to support its agenda, was quite unlike anything witnessed before.

What has in recent times helped turn the diaspora into ambassadors of nationalism was the growing narrative of India as a 'Vishwa Guru' and Prime Minister Modi as the shaper of the new world order. Additionally, global interventions such as bringing back stranded Indians during the Ukraine conflict or

India's initiative to send vaccines across the world during the Covid-19 pandemic, had resulted in Narendra Modi's image soaring. What added to the clout were events such as those organized by the OFBJP in several US states demanding the international isolation of Pakistan after the Pulwama attacks. It helped that various surveys also showed PM Modi being among the most powerful world leaders. In fact, a survey conducted by US-based consultancy firm Morning Consult released in December 2023 showed Prime Minister Modi acquiring the top position as the world's most popular leader with an approval rating of 76 per cent.[1]

Observers credit this in part to PM Modi's ability to connect with people. Says Akashika Mohla, an Australia-based media, policy, advocacy and international affairs expert, who recalls how the visits of PM Modi to Australia stirred a spectrum of emotions. 'When PM Modi visited Australia, it felt like a piece of home had arrived on foreign shores. His presence brought a sense of connection to my Indian heritage while navigating the nuances of being an Australian. It was a moment of pride, yet also a reminder of the balancing act we often perform in a cultural context where we sometimes feel like outsiders. Our PM Albanese's reference to PM Modi as "the boss" during his visit felt like a validation of the influence and respect our Indian heritage holds in Australia. When I think about PM Modi's leadership and India's role in the region, it feels like a guiding light shining on the path to a more secure and prosperous future,' she adds.

Having covered the prime minister on his multiple foreign trips starting with his first in 2014 for G20 in Australia, we have witnessed a similar fervour and connection. In November 2014 when the prime minister arrived in Australia, he was the first Indian prime minister in twenty-eight years to visit the country. Big posters hailing him as 'Rockstar Modi' had been put up outside Allphones Arena—the venue of the reception organized by the Indian community. While addressing the diaspora, PM Modi referred to Swami Vivekananda's dream of seeing India as a Vishwa Guru before adding that he believed that the dream would soon be a reality. Do you share the dream, he asked thousands of cheering people in the arena. He also invited the Indian-Australian community to give back to the motherland in whatever way they could. This idea of giving back to the motherland would play out in all the countries that Modi would subsequently travel to. As India's graph rose, what also grew was the sense of pride and commitment among the NRIs. In 2022 when we travelled to cover the Quadrilateral Security Dialogue (Quad) summit in Tokyo, we witnessed a supremely confident Indian community present outside the hotel where the prime minister was staying. Amitabh Kumar Singh, a Bihari by birth, who had settled in Tokyo and ran a chain of restaurants in several cities in Japan, summarized what several people of Indian origin in Japan were feeling: 'Earlier, nobody took note of Indian contributions, but the story is different now. PM Modi meets us every time he is in Japan and ensures that we get our due in the foreign country and also in India.' The pride was palpable when he pointed out that 'the older generation of NRIs speak about other PMs who had nearly forgotten Indians abroad; but this PM is different. He not only tells us our worth but makes countries realize how NRIs are valuable to those countries.'

What has emerged as a result of all these factors is what Badri Narayan, a social historian and author, calls 'a phase characterized by a sense of global nationalism', one that he feels has been 'propelled by the power of social media, the expansive reach of cyber spaces, and the burgeoning global sense of nationalism.'

This is not to say that PM Modi does not have critics overseas. While his supporters credit him with ensuring that

India has got its due on the global stage, his critics equally accuse him of promoting Hindu nationalism. 'We claim as a diaspora we're very connected to our heritage and we want to celebrate our culture,' Harita Iswara, twenty-three, was quoted as saying to the NBC. 'But when people's identities are under attack in India, we have to do as much, if not more, to speak up to protect them.'[2] Iswara was among the many who staged a protest during PM Modi's visit to the US. It deserves a mention that at a news conference held jointly with Joe Biden in 2023, when PM Modi was categorically asked about the claims that his government is known to discriminate against religious minorities, his response—'I'm actually really surprised that people say so. Indeed, India is a democracy. We have always proved that democracy can deliver. And when I say deliver, this is regardless of caste, creed, religion, gender. There's absolutely no space for discrimination'[3]—met with thunderous applause from his supporters. Ironically though, Sabrina Siddiqui, the reporter for *The Wall Street Journal* who had raised the question, was swiftly attacked on social media, highlighting her Muslim heritage and connections to Pakistan, with Twitter handles labelling her as a 'Pakistani Islamist'. Siddiqui's wasn't a one-off case. Activists working in the space have time and again pointed out the vile slurs and threats they have been facing. The issues of discrimination raised by critics have also been reflected in several recent rankings of the country that have raised concern. In 2021, the US-based not-for-profit Freedom House downgraded India's status from a free democracy to a 'partially free democracy' while the Economist Intelligence Unit categorized India as a 'flawed democracy'.[4]

PM Modi's supporters, however, are quick to dismiss these charges and offer what they consider is clinching evidence that runs contrary to the charges of discrimination. Pointing to his chemistry with both President Trump and President Biden, they feel that PM Modi needs to be acknowledged for his non-alignment. They also point out that he needs to be applauded for creating history in becoming only the third Indian leader to make a state visit to the US and the only Indian prime minister to address a joint session of the US Congress twice. In fact, his address to the joint session even saw US lawmakers seeking autographs from PM Modi.

Impact on Home Turf

The difference in opinion between his supporters and detractors apart, diaspora nationalism has had a far-reaching impact on domestic politics as well. It stands to reason that a significant change has come by way of the fact that while global events and diplomacy did not reach the common people earlier, PM Modi and the BJP have succeeded in bringing it down to the grassroots level. PM Modi's large rallies in foreign countries and India's intervention in many important global events are seen as a sign of the country's growing strength. Even a cursory check will reveal that pre-2014, diplomatic tours of prime ministers were rarely a mainstream televised event. In the post 2014 era, every visit of the prime minister from Australia to Denmark to the Middle East and of course to the United States was not only covered extensively but also projected as India negotiating with the world on its own terms. 'Some of these overseas events have been designed as spectacles. Even when they are taking place in the US or Australia or anywhere else, they are as much for the consumption of the domestic audience in India. Prime Minister Modi's ability to use these kinds of platforms to reach out to Indian voters remains phenomenal,' opines political analyst Rahul Verma.

Conversations with a cross section of India's voters ratify Verma's theory. 'When Manmohan Singh used to go abroad, nobody would come to see him. Nobody even knew about it. India's presence was not felt. Now, look, when our Prime Minister Narendra Modi goes to any corner of the world, crowds gather just to see him. More people gather in any country around the world to hear Modi than those who come to see Manmohan Singh in Darbhanga. Seeing this, one realizes how much our status has increased in the world. Now, India has strength,' says retired teacher Ramsavek Jha from Darbhanga, Bihar. Jha is not alone in feeling the way he does.

In 2019, just before the General Elections, we undertook a train journey to understand the mood of India's voters. Aboard the Kamakhya Express, covering 3100 kilometres from Ahmedabad to Kamakhya, passing through six states, we had a range of conversations with fellow passengers, among whom was Mithilesh Meena from Rajasthan's Kota. While he mentioned facing many challenges personally on account of lack of development, he was happy that India had now become a global leader. The forty-five-minute conversation was punctuated with him playing several videos that he had received on WhatsApp. One such video showed PM Modi meeting Facebook founder Zuckerberg in America. Meena's premise was that when India's esteem rises on the world stage, development is bound to follow.

Narendra Modi's increasing recognition worldwide and its impact on India's rising graph in the world is more than Meena's singular opinion. As a matter of fact, the impact of global diplomacy is being increasingly observed on domestic politics. It is a testimony to BJP's success that the Opposition, which was initially critical of PM Modi's frequent foreign tours, has followed suit in trying to woo the diaspora. Recognizing the strength of the NRI community, the Congress Party, for instance, has formed several committees to strengthen their hold among the diasporas. Rahul Gandhi, a senior leader of the Indian National Congress Party, has been jetting across the US to interact with the Indian diaspora. From interacting with students at the prestigious Stanford University to having meetings with lawmakers and think tanks and addressing a public gathering, his visits are said to be aimed at promoting shared values and a vision of 'real democracy'. Indian Overseas Congress chairman Sam Pitroda was quoted as saying that the purpose of Gandhi's trip was 'to connect, interact and begin a new conversation with various individuals, institutions and media, including the Indian diaspora that is growing in numbers in the United States and abroad'.[5] The same is true of the AAP, a relative upstart in the political sphere but which is backed by what University of California, Santa Barbara, scholar Shinder S. Thandi called, 'the powerful "non-state actors" of Punjab; its redoubtable emigrants, with foreign passports and citizenships but a deep connect with the state's politics'.[6] With the ruling party pushing hard to open up avenues for the diaspora to exercise their influence in Indian politics it stands to reason that both global nationalism and vibrant expat politics are slated to grow.

Remember, Mahatma Gandhi was also an NRI, absentee NRI voting rights campaigners have been reminding everyone time and again. Seems like 'Never underestimate an NRI'—is a mantra for all parties.

To Sum Up

It is important to remember that the dynamics of global diplomacy often unfold in unexpected ways, where the stakes can sometimes also be reversed. Diplomacy is said to operate silently, minimizing the possibility of overt confrontation. However, when global diplomacy engages with a country's audience, the stakes for it to always emerge unscathed increase significantly. Instances such as the alleged accusations against

India's investigation agency by the United States in the case of Sikh separatist Pannu's assassination or tensions with Canada, highlighted not just diplomatic intricacies but also political constraints. Such sensitive incidents showcased the pressure of global multilateralism.

Similarly, while India was dubbed a 'Vishwa Guru', analysts noted how the term appeared incongruous on the global stage. Consequently, leaders such as PM Narendra Modi and other responsible figures opted to reframe it as 'Vishwa Bandhu' or 'Vishwa Mitra', emphasizing a more egalitarian and collaborative global role for India. This strategic shift acknowledged the nuances of international relations, where perceptions can significantly impact diplomatic outcomes. The evolving narrative underscores how countries navigate their global image amidst intricate diplomatic manoeuvres, balancing national interests with global expectations. As India continues to assert its presence on the world stage, the adaptation of new terminology reflects a pragmatic approach to diplomatic engagement, resonating more effectively with diverse global audiences.

Chapter 6

Political Tricolour and Soft Hindutva

Time: Sometime in 2019

Place: A WhatsApp group of friends

Adnan: Not sure how all of you will take my comments but the political situation really worries me. Over the last five years the BJP has polarized votes to such an extent that political parties are shying away from giving tickets to Muslim candidates. I mean they feel just by doing it, it will cost them the Hindu vote bank.

Ahmed: You are right, the Congress, in particular, has reduced the number of tickets to Muslims due to fear that it will backfire electorally.

Ahmed: I think the fault also lay in the fact that the Congress looked at Muslims only as a 'vote bank' and did little to promote leadership within the community.

This WhatsApp group is demonstrative of the popular outpourings and messages that were in circulation during these events. The participants in the chat are fictional. Any similarity to actual persons, living or dead, is purely coincidental.

Mohammad Ashfaq: I don't even think it is just a Muslim issue. I think the Congress, for one, needs to rethink its politics not just for the sake of Muslims but to salvage its own image as a party that is committed to the constitutional principles of secularism and pluralism.

Hasan: Whatever it is, I hope good sense prevails sooner rather than later and as a country we do not lose our pluralistic ethos.

* * *

Hobson's Choice

'Some sections of society have an impression that the party is inclined to certain communities or organizations. Congress policy is equal justice to everyone. But people have doubts whether that policy is being implemented or not. This doubt is created by the party's proximity towards minority communities,'[1] A.K. Antony, veteran Congress leader, said.

After the Congress Party faced a resounding defeat in the 2014 Lok Sabha elections, being relegated to as low as forty-four seats, a review committee set up under A.K. Antony's leadership found minority appeasement to be one of the major causes of its electoral loss. It was found that a significant section of Hindus felt that most non-BJP parties overlooked their interests and focused mainly on minorities. It didn't help that the BJP seemed to be advancing the notion that the Congress Party and the other so-called secular parties engaged in religious pandering to secure their Muslim vote bank in the garb of secularism. Post the 2014 elections, it stands to reason then that there was little talk of secularism by parties as there was the potent fear of being labelled 'minority appeasers'. From the A.K. Antony report to the more recent Raipur Plenary of the Congress Party (the 85th plenary session of the Congress that concluded in Raipur in Chhattisgarh outlined a strategy for the 2024 Lok Sabha election) 'how to remove the anti-Hindu tag' has been a key focus area within the Congress. The obvious solution was to pivot to brandish their own Hindu credentials to blunt the BJP's appeal. In the words of political activist Yogendra Yadav, 'Secular politics faced a Hobson's choice: it could take a "hard" line and face electoral marginalization. Or it could go for "soft Hindutva" and betray its cause.'[2]

Whether it meant betraying their cause or not, most opposition parties chose the latter. While it may seem ironic that the cure for the BJP's marginalization of the Muslims was to make the Congress more Hindu, the Congress Party's manifesto in Madhya Pradesh in 2018 included setting up *gaushala*s, or cow shelters, in each of the state's 23,000 panchayats; it also committed itself to developing the *Ram Van Gaman Path,* or the route that was taken by Lord Rama on his way to exile that was widely revered by Hindus.

Despite these sporadic efforts, the 2019 Lok Sabha polls turned out to be an encore for the BJP, with it garnering the highest-ever national vote share. According to Lokniti-CSDS' post-poll survey for the 2019 elections, the BJP and its allies managed to secure close to 52 per cent of the Hindu votes all over India, the highest consolidation of Hindu votes nationally in three decades. Intriguingly, the oath-taking ceremony for members of Parliament to the seventeenth Lok Sabha was drowned in shouts of '*Jai Shri Ram*'; the chant particularly gaining decibels during the oath-taking of specific members of the Opposition.

With the BJP's thumping majority, the question, that if voters could vote for the real Hindutva party, why would they choose an unequal match in other parties, seemed to have become a rhetorical one. Some voices within the Congress

Party also wondered if their efforts were leading them to become a poor copy of the BJP. Political observers, however, opine that the party's assertion of Hindu credentials is not so much a bid to woo the majority community but an attempt to shed the pro-minority image and take the sting out of the BJP's campaign. In other words, the pro-Hindu strategy isn't aimed at winning votes, but to avoid losing them. By repeatedly showcasing their religiosity in full public view, the opposition leaders are keen to cancel out the 'anti-Hindu' barbs of the BJP. Whether it was Kamal Nath declaring himself to be a 'Hanuman bhakta', or Rahul Gandhi's temple appearances with a smear of sandalwood paste and a thick run of holy ash on his forehead, or Priyanka Gandhi offering prayers to the Narmada river, or Akhilesh Yadav's temple-hopping spree from Ayodhya to Chitrakoot, or Arvind Kejriwal reciting the Hanuman Chalisa—leaders in the opposition parties continued to make every effort to prove their Hindu credentials and ensure public outreach. Among the instances that particularly stand out as a testimony to the efforts of countering the BJP's Hindutva rhetoric was the cautious opposition to the five-judge bench's unanimous verdict on the Ram Temple (the Supreme Court ordered the disputed land to be handed over to a trust to build the Ram Janmabhoomi temple) which came close on the heels of the 2019 Lok Sabha verdict. In the more recent concluding address to the Bharat Jodo Yatra (a 3570-km journey that began at Kanniyakumari on 7 September 2022, and ended at Srinagar and which was the Congress Party's biggest mass contact programme in the recent times led by former party president Rahul Gandhi), while Rahul Gandhi spoke against BJP's majoritarian politics, analysts opine that he reasserted his Hindu identity and Pandit lineage, a testimony to the Congress Party's belief that their return to power could be on the back of the theme of Hindu pride.

Speak to opposition leaders, however, and they believe that the accusation of the Opposition engaging in 'soft Hindutva' is fundamentally wrong. Speaking to Madhya Pradesh's former chief minister Kamal Nath during his campaign trail in Datia during the 2023 assembly elections, where he visited the Pitambara Peeth, Mr Nath told us his devotion cannot be seen as recent as he had done the *pran pratishtha* of the 101-foot idol of Lord Hanuman as far back as December 2014 and that religiosity has been very integral to him.

In the 2023 Assembly elections, the then Chhattisgarh chief minister and Congress leader Bhupesh Baghel similarly refuted the soft Hindutva charge while referring to the history of the Congress Party. Mahatma Gandhi, he explained, always sang *'Raghupati Raghav Raja Ram'* and Lokmanya Tilak unified the youth through Ganesh puja during the fight for independence. 'Ram belongs to us, Ganesh belongs to us,' he passionately explained. 'What is RSS's swadeshi? Gandhi's entire movement was about that. The movement to burn foreign clothes was ours, so how did we become "soft"?' he asks. K.C. Tyagi, former member of Parliament and JDU leader, similarly explains that religion, nation and related sentiments don't come from a party's perspective. 'Religion is a personal sentiment, personal faith, and we have practised politics for five decades with this understanding. In the era of media and social media, some people have tried to create narratives according to their beliefs, and they found some success in that,' he adds. He sounds a note of caution in saying that 'more than the Opposition, society needs introspection. Society needs to answer whether the entry of religion into politics is right or not, because if politics also gets completely filled with religious activities, then where will other fundamental issues find space?'

Hinduism Not Hindutva

Amidst criticism around the fact that if the BJP is programmatically communal, opposition parties are pragmatically so, many opposition leaders echo Tyagi's views that religion is a matter of personal faith and have gone to great lengths to clarify that burnishing their Hindu credentials isn't akin to going against their grain. It has been contended time and again by members of the Congress Party that Hinduism is not the same as Hindutva and that the Congress has no issue with the former. Congress MP and author of *Why I Am a Hindu*, Shashi Tharoor, argues in his book that Hindutva is a gross perversion of Hindu spirituality. He had earlier made his point in a tweet that 'Hinduism is the union of various Indian cultures and traditions with diverse roots and no founder, while Hindutva is a homogenous racial-territorial category propagated by Savarkar'.[3, 4] He went to explain the difference further as he was quoted as saying that 'Hinduism is a very large, eclectic, vastly encompassing religion that has a tremendous amount of choice of freedom within it, which is actually one of the greatest strengths of Hinduism. The problem with Hindutva is that it takes this vast all-encompassing religion and tries to reduce it to something much narrower and specifically tie it to a political identity.'

Rahul Gandhi has also on several occasions drawn a distinction between Hinduism as an inclusive religion and Hindutva as a militant political ideology. To call 'Hinduism a set of cultural norms is to misunderstand it', and 'to bind it to a particular nation or geography is to limit it,' Gandhi wrote in a piece in the *Indian Express*.[5] 'Hinduism', Gandhi says, 'is how we mitigate and understand our relationship with our fears.

It is a path towards the realization of truth and though it belongs
to no one, it is open to anyone who chooses to walk on it.'
Going by this differentiation, visiting temples or participating
in Hindu rituals does not count as pandering to soft Hindutva.

Critics, however, point out that in trying to beat the BJP
at its own game by using Hinduism and not Hindutva as its
shield, Congress and other parties stand not just to lose their
own identity, they also run the risk of throwing the minorities
under the bus for fear of offending the majority. It has been
pointed out that it is a slippery slope as it is likely to erode the
ground under their feet, not to mention the fact that the price
of such a strategy would also be the fear and insecurity of the
minority communities. Several examples have been pointed out
that give credence to this fear. Delhi's Chief Minister Arvind
Kejriwal, for instance, came under fire for his silence during
the 2020 north-east Delhi riots. Similarly, in 2022 when the
BJP-controlled municipal corporation bulldozed the mostly
Muslim-owned properties in Delhi's Jahangirpuri, the Congress
was conspicuous by its absence, while the AAP tried to get out
of the situation by referring to the victims as 'Bangladeshis' and
'Rohingyas'.

There, of course, are no easy political answers, as in
contemporary India even those opposed to the politics of
communalization argue that religion is too powerful a resource
to be ignored. In other words, even if there are more pressing
issues such as the economy and unemployment, majoritarian
politics is the elephant in the room that cannot be ignored.
Several analysts feel that what is happening is only natural, given
the fact that the party in power typically has an advantage in
terms of setting the agenda and every other party is compelled to
carve its distinct identity within the broader national narrative.
'In any sort of dominant party system this is likely to happen.
What we are witnessing therefore is that the Opposition parties

are trying to mirror the dominant party in strategy and tactics. So, at this moment everyone will try to be seen as a little bit of a pro Hindu and pro nationalist, because if you are seen as being weak on these two fronts you may actually face a backlash. So yes, in the short and medium run nationalism is going to stay unless the Opposition parties figure out a narrative and mobilize on issues that are much stronger for them and weaker for the BJP. If they manage to open up a space on economic uncertainty, if they manage to open up a space on social justice politics, then certainly they can bring down the scenes of nationalism at least in the medium term,' opines political analyst Rahul Verma.

Critics like Zafar Sareshwala, however, differ, and see this pro-Hindu posturing by the non-BJP parties as being completely ineffective. 'If Congress Party is doing what BJP is doing then I will call them a B team of BJP. If I have to select a Hindu then I will select Modi-Shah. The Congress Party or any opposition has to come out with its own narrative. This will not work,' he says on the efficacy of the soft Hindutva plank. He goes on to add an important proviso that the 'Hindutva plank is working only with jobs and development. Hindutva alone doesn't work. Look at Pakistan. None of the religious parties have got more than 8 per cent votes. The only exception being 2001-2002 when all these religious parties came together and formed a government. Religious fervour alone can't work. It can only act as a spice. But if the food itself isn't right then all this spicing up doesn't work,' he says, implying that the BJP has multiple planks other than Hindutva.

Sareshwala's comment on the balance between faith and economy seemed to come alive during our reportage of the 2023 Madhya Pradesh assembly elections when we travelled to Ujjain. Mahakal Lok—the magnificent corridor surrounding the historic Mahakaleshwar Temple—was inaugurated by Prime Minister Modi on 11 October 2022, which has given the temple town a massive infrastructure push. At the majestic Mahakal corridor, we met seventy-year-old Kamala Bai who started a kurtas and scarves stall one year ago. She mentioned that it is because of the temple that her life has changed forever. Though only the first phase of the temple corridor development project has been unveiled, the footfall of devotees has increased multifold, touching a whopping 1.5 lakh to 2.5 lakh on weekends. This means good business for many like Pradeep Goswami who runs a guest house and Deepak Kohli who started his own laundry business, quitting his salaried job of Rs 10,000 a month. 'I quit my job and started this as I realized that hotels would need some set-up to get their bed sheets and other linens washed daily.' The economies of temple towns such as Kashi, Ujjain and now Ayodhya, have changed dramatically. What this has brought in its wake is undoubtable faith in the BJP and PM Modi that he can bring a balance between faith and economy.

Coming back to the electoral viability of the Hindutva stand of Opposition parties, researcher and historian Nikhil Menon raises a pertinent question—'The costs of a fraying social fabric and vitiated politics aside, is it even likely to succeed electorally in the long term? Modern Indian history suggests otherwise.' Before we conclude, it will be worthwhile then to delve a little into the history of the intertwined world of religion and politics in India.

The World of Religion and Politics

The coming together of religion and politics is hardly new in India.

Even though most popular discussions on nationalism and Hindutva tend to centre on the BJP's electoral resurgence in 2014, the fact is that the Hindutva movement has a long lineage. A major milestone in the journey of Hindu nationalism was, of course, the formation of the RSS in 1925, which aimed to strengthen Hindu society and unify Hindus. Hindu nationalism in its current avatar, however, has been credited to Savarkar and his maxim of 'Hindu, Hindi, Hindustan', which emphasized a sense of nationalism based on religious identity.

While it is widely believed that India's post-1947 identity essentially took on a secular cast under the Congress Party, social commentators say that this isn't necessarily true. Researchers point out that the Bharat Sadhu Samaj, for instance, was established as early as 1956, under the Congress watch, based on the belief that the ascetics would help popularize the five-year plans among the Hindus. In 1989, the Sadhu Samaj, however, turned on its parent, informally aligning itself with the Vishva Hindu Parishad (VHP) and BJP.

Social expert and psephologist Yashwant Deshmukh goes a step further and draws our attention to the fact that 'our habit has become that we see the history of India from 1947 and the electoral history from 1952. Whereas that's not true. The electoral history starts from 1926. At that time, the Congress did not participate in the elections and allowed its leaders to contest elections as small groups. Even within the Congress, there appeared two factions—soft and hard factions, popularly known as Garam Dal and Naram Dal, which were different versions of secular and right-wing. By 1936, the Muslim League also emerged. That's when politics based on religion started. The foundation of division was formed amidst this politics. Then we accepted a Muslim country, Pakistan, and a secular country, India. However, there was resentment among Hindus who remained in India after the division based on religion. This resentment grew after independence. But after Mahatma Gandhi's death, it turned into a temporary pause. Hindus were in guilt after Gandhi's murder. It didn't mean that the anger that arose among the people had ended at that time. Somewhere within the Hindus of the country, there was a sense of being ignored. One could say that the issue of Hindu identity was bound to come up sooner or later, and that's what we are witnessing nowadays. Suppressed emotions have surfaced. It could be said that the guilt of seven decades has somehow ended for Hindus,' he opines. 'The impact of nationalism or Hindutva always remains hidden or active in politics. We assess it differently based on different times,' Deshmukh adds.

Noted author and columnist Nilanjan Mukhopadhyay similarly argues that there was a 'latent sentiment in India which was unarticulated'—namely that the Muslims who desired a separate nation had been granted one, and those who had stayed must conform to the majority's terms. This perspective, described as 'soft Hindutva', gained traction over time, becoming more openly expressed. 'These sentiments, initially unarticulated, gained momentum through movements like the Ram Janmabhoomi movement and then eventually, a time came when it (the viewpoint) was considered to be not politically incorrect anymore,' Mukhopadhyay says. Mukhopadhyay also makes an interesting point about the tricolour when he points out that the Indian tricolour had always been on display, even through the 50s, 60s and 70s. However, it was absent from Hindu right-wing organizations. 'It was quite late when they realized that they could not make an entry into the Indian national political space unless they started appropriating the national movement and all symbols which are considered to be Indian. It is a very conscious choice which has been made slowly over the decades. Not everything has been done post 2014,' Mukhopadhyay concludes.

Competitive Religiosity

Quoting a Supreme Court judgment, PM Modi while on a visit to Canada had stated, 'Hindu dharam is not a religion but a way of life.' In the current times, it sure seems like the two variants of Hindu nationalism—the BJP's Hindutva plank and the softer variant of Hindutva or Hinduism as espoused by the other parties—have become a way of life and are here to stay. A big case in point was seen in the BJP's launch of its 2024 election campaign centred on nationalism and Hindutva. This initiative saw opposition parties taking a calculated political risk by abstaining from major events such as the inauguration of the Ram Temple in Ayodhya. This decision sent a strong message, underscored by opinion polls, indicating potential heavy losses for the Opposition.

Amidst the fervent cries of '*Jai Shri Ram*' and '*Bharat Mata ki Jai*', the BJP surged forward with determined vigour to sideline the Opposition entirely. At the same time, the Opposition countered it with their own narrative, embracing a novel interpretation of Hindutva and nationalism. They accused the BJP of excessively prioritizing religion and patriotism at the expense of other critical issues. This accusation resonated with sections of the public, leading to pockets of success.

As for the political landscape, it became a battleground of ideologies, where both sides strategically manoeuvred to sway public sentiment amidst a backdrop of nationalistic fervour and identity politics. The general election promised to be a crucial test of these competing narratives, shaping the future trajectory of Indian politics.

In conclusion, the election results have proven that the country is indeed diverse. The meanings of Hindutva or nationalism were therefore perceived differently state by state, and community by community. The election results have also

shown that where the Opposition appeared confused, the BJP
fell victim to overconfidence. Importantly, the results have also
proven that in the coming years, all parties will need to better
connect with the public on issues, which are not just related to
their emotions but also to practical concerns.

Chapter 7

Reimagining the Poll Plan

Time: February 2024

Place: WhatsApp group of friends

Arjun: What a moment for Indians! PM Modi just inaugurated the grand BAPS Hindu temple in Abu Dhabi.

Ashish: Yes, India is clearly having a moment on the world stage. Who but Modi could have made this possible? He seems to be on a roll. Just a few weeks ago he presided over the consecration ceremony of the grand Ram Temple in Ayodhya.

Vikas: The Emirates are home to about 3.6 million Indians. I can't even imagine how proud they must be feeling.

Sankalp: Sorry to be a party pooper. I recognize these patriotic feelings and how proud we are feeling as Hindus, but surely

---

This WhatsApp group is demonstrative of the popular outpourings and messages that were in circulation during these events. The participants in the chat are fictional. Any similarity to actual persons, living or dead, is purely coincidental.

you all can see that his mega Gulf outreach continues unabated in preparation for a third electoral term.

Arjun: What is wrong with that? As long as he is doing everything possible to deepen ties with other countries and also bringing pride to our own country.

Ashish: Besides, he had put in a request to Sheikh Mohamed bin Zayed, then crown prince of Abu Dhabi, as early as 2015 to grant some land for the temple.

Arjun: I just think it is fashionable to criticize the government, and you, my friend, seem to be taking the bait. Let's not discuss this any further.

* * *

Diaspora Connect

In February 2024, Prime Minister Modi was all set to make his last diplomatic visit to the United Arab Emirates (UAE) before the world's largest democracy going to polls. Set to address the 'Ahlan Modi' event at Zayed Sports City Stadium in Abu Dhabi, and also to inaugurate the Bochasanwasi Akshar Purushottam Swaminarayan Sanstha (BAPS) Mandir, the first traditional Hindu temple in the UAE, the visit was his seventh to the UAE since 2015 and the third in the previous eight months.

'This is the time to hail the friendship between India and the UAE. In this historic stadium, every heartbeat echoes the same sentiment. Long live Bharat-UAE friendship,'[1] PM Modi said at the event, which began with the national anthems of the two countries. 'I have come to meet my family,' he told the

Indian diaspora, adding that he had brought the fragrance of the soil where they were born. There were words of praise for President Sheikh Mohamed bin Zayed Al Nahyan, whom the prime minister has repeatedly referred to as his 'brother', for his contribution to the growing partnership. PM Modi also stated that what India and the UAE had achieved in terms of community integration was a model for the whole world. Amidst loud cheers, he pointed out that the inauguration of a Hindu temple in Abu Dhabi was a 'historic moment' and that the friendship between the two countries would live long and continue to prosper. Earlier in January 2024, amidst deepening ties between India and the UAE, Prime Minister Modi had greeted UAE President Sheikh Mohamed bin Zayed Al Nahyan with a grand welcome at Ahmedabad in India, which had set the stage for showcasing the strong bonds of friendship and cooperation between the two nations.

'Third Term' Pitch

At Ahlan Modi, not only did PM Modi praise the growing synergy between India and the UAE, he also spoke of the direction it would take in his 'third term'. 'Modi *ki guarantee* means *guarantee pura hone ki guarantee* (Modi's guarantee means that every guarantee will be met),' he declared. His optimism was mirrored by the thousands of expat Indians who were attending the event despite inclement weather conditions. Speaking to us, the members of the diaspora pointed out how the way Indians are treated has completely changed. 'We are proud Indians—we are recognized; we are given opportunities,' they said before breaking into chants of '*Modi hai toh mumkin hai* and *Bharat UAE dosti zindabad*,' Modi makes the impossible, possible; long live India–UAE friendship.

Eighty-three-year-old Mohan Valrani, the founding vice chairman of the Al Shirawi Group, was one of the few people who was part of the contingent that had received PM Indira Gandhi when she had made a visit to the UAE in 1981. 'After that visit, we haven't had any prime minister visit us till ten years ago,' he points out. 'I salute PM Modi. What he has achieved is unbelievable.' Having moved to the UAE in 1966 with seven dollars in his pocket, Valrani has witnessed a lot of changes. 'We do not feel like second-class citizens any more. There is a lot of respect for Indians,' he explains. His son, fifty-two-year-old Navin Valrani, also goes on to talk about the Emirates–India camaraderie. 'PM Modi leads a life of integrity, discipline and deep humility. In the UAE he made us believe that if we aim for the stars, we will get the stars.'

Valrani's words are echoed by Surendra Kandhari, a first-generation resident of Dubai who runs the Guru Nanak Darbar Gurudwara at Jebel Ali. In fact, the place is a spiritual oasis of tolerance hidden amidst the glitzy skyscrapers of Dubai where a gurudwara, church and temple stand next to each other. 'The rulers of the UAE believe in inclusiveness and diversity,' he points out before going on to add that Indians are today trusted because of Modi. 'He is a star of stars, very charismatic; he has changed the face of India and Indians across the world.'

PM Modi's visit to Abu Dhabi to inaugurate the biggest Hindu temple in west Asia of course had a huge connect with Indians. A Muslim king donating land for a Hindu temple where the lead architect was a Catholic, the project manager a Sikh, the foundational designer a Buddhist, the construction company a Parsi group and the director coming from the Jain tradition, did indeed send a message of ultimate harmony and coexistence.

Speaking of what makes the BAPS temple unique, Sunjay Sudhir, ambassador of India to the UAE, points out that, 'The temple comes out of the vision of the two leaders.

It was announced after PM Modi visited the UAE in 2015. The temple saw twenty-seven acres of land being given by the UAE government and the largest involvement of the Indian community.' Speaking of the relation between the two countries, he further goes on to add how the Comprehensive Economic Partnership Agreement (CEPA) between the Government of the Republic of India and the Government of the UAE was inked during the Covid-19 pandemic. 'The strength of the relationship came out loud and clear,' he adds.

Getting back to the temple, the excitement ahead of its inauguration, which marked a significant milestone in the cultural landscape of Abu Dhabi, was palpable. Open to people of all faiths, the BAPS Hindu temple rises from the UAE's desertscape as a symbol of cross-cultural harmony. The first Hindu temple in the Middle East to be built using traditional Indian techniques, it is also the region's biggest. Built at an estimated cost of Dh400 million, the temple's significance extends beyond its architectural grandeur, embodying a message of harmony and collaboration between India and the Gulf region.

Ahead of the inauguration, Prime Minister Modi offered water in the virtual Ganga and Yamuna rivers in the temple premises and then proceeded to offer prayers inside the temple. The guest list for the inauguration ceremony included Indian government officials, Bollywood stars and members of illustrious business families. Senior Abu Dhabi officials were also in attendance.

The inauguration of the 108-foot-high temple marked a pinnacle for the Hindu community in the UAE, as well as for the two countries' bilateral ties, which PM Modi will hope to capitalize on if he returns with a majority.

* * *

Sabka Sath—The Domestic Scenario

Soon after he was elected the leader of the BJP parliamentary party for the second term, Prime Minister Narendra Modi coined a new slogan: '*sabka sath, sabka vikas, sabka vishwas*', together with all, development for all, the trust of all.

'Today I appeal to all that we have to break that deceit on minorities. We have to gain their trust. We have to move shoulder to shoulder without discriminating on the basis of caste, sect and religion. We are for 130 crore people. These should be our priorities and responsibility. *Sabka sath, sabka vikas aur ab sabka vishwas.* This is our mantra. I will leave no stone unturned and I will work for all citizens of India,' he had said during his address to BJP MPs in the central hall of Parliament.[2]

When it was time to pitch for an important third electoral term, not only did the BJP's minority outreach once again take centre stage, but one of the focus areas of the campaign was the welfare schemes for different sections of society. In fact, the PM emphasized in multiple rallies held in the months leading up to the general election that the lotus, the party's symbol, should be the only candidate for all workers of the party—thus making each candidate replaceable, with none having the entitlement to demand tickets. While dropping MPs and MLAs to beat anti-incumbency has been one of the formulae of success for Modi since his chief ministerial days, this time, there was also a focus on replacing candidates that had crossed the line by making statements that were anti-minority and brought embarrassment to the party leadership.

This is particularly important since the BJP had earlier faced harsh criticism for its handling of minority issues. An example being that of a cacophonous TV debate that had witnessed objectionable and communal statements, ultimately leading to the suspension of the BJP's spokesperson Nupur Sharma and its media cell head, Naveen Kumar. The controversy, however, took an unprecedented turn when a diplomatic furore broke out in the Gulf countries, and India's secular credentials and its plurality were put to the test on the world stage. So much so that there was also a call to boycott Indian products in the Gulf countries. Clearly, there was too much at stake for India, with India's trade with the Gulf Cooperation Council (GCC) standing at a whopping $87 billion in 2020–21.

Back home, the Opposition was also quick to accuse the BJP of defaming India at the international level and maintained that it had to apologize for its mistakes. While the Congress on its official Twitter handle said that 'the BJP has gone so far in its deceitfulness, arrogance, and pride, that it has become blind in its own darkness. The consequences of the BJP's actions are its own to pay, not the nation's'.[3] Rahul Gandhi was also quoted as saying, 'The atmosphere in the country has been created by the ruling dispensation. It is not the person who has made the comment. It is the Prime Minister. It is the Home Minister. It's the BJP and the RSS. It's an anti-national act.'[4]

As the backlash threatened to upend relationships and key alliances, the BJP issued suspension orders for Nupur Sharma, besides placing on record its statement that it respects all religions and strongly denounces insults of any religious personality. Despite this, most people felt that the fact that it took Qatar and Kuwait to get the Government of India to respond indicated a moral and humanitarian lapse. In other words, it was felt that trade ties had won over humanity, else an episode of this kind shouldn't have needed a prod from an ally in the Gulf. In short, most saw the suspension as a mere 'damage-control' exercise for the sake of international optics.

Nilanjan Mukhopadhyay, eminent author and writer, in speaking to us points out that 'following that incident, we've seen numerous instances where hate speech or statements targeting minorities continued persistently. Throughout various elections, we've witnessed statements from party leaders. Had these statements been made by leaders of the Opposition, they would have been imprisoned. Yes, in the case of Nupur Sharma, the BJP's actions were influenced by international pressure, necessitating some form of action as a global image-saving strategy for the government,' he says. Giving specific instances, he adds that 'Post-2014, there were statements that were more incendiary, one after another. Remember Sadhvi Niranjana Jyoti's statement? At the same time, Yogi Adityanath made controversial remarks that incited issues, leading to internal discussions and even attacks within the country. It reached a point where even President Obama had to address it. This incident was seen as a moment where pressure surfaced, leading to some action. However, at the party level, there wasn't a sincere effort to discard such statements. If there had been sincerity, the government would have sent these people to jail, sending a firm message against such statements. Such actions could have been taken to establish a lasting deterrent against such hate speech,' he points out.

BJP MP Zafar Islam, however, has a different opinion and points out that there have been many instances in the past where the party has taken disciplinary action. 'I must tell you that if somebody crosses the red line, then the party definitely has a disciplinary committee which swings into action. It is not one of those isolated events. There are many such instances where the party has taken a call based on certain remarks made by a political leader, a party leader and party leadership as well as the disciplinary committee felt that they should be discussed in the disciplinary committee and eventually whatever the disciplinary committee felt and recommended to the leadership has been implemented,' he points out.

In the run-up to the 2024 elections, this seemed to ring true as the BJP's strategy was to consciously drop motormouths. It recognized the potential dangers lurking within the realm of religious rhetoric, as witnessed by the fact that the party denied tickets to leaders like Pragya Thakur and Ramesh Bidhuri, whose statements in the months prior to the General Elections had courted controversy. Thakur had run into trouble with her party, including Prime Minister Modi, over her controversial remarks regarding Nathuram Godse. Similarly, Ramesh Bidhuri was one among the four sitting MPs to be denied a ticket after making offensive remarks against Bahujan Samaj Party MP Danish Ali in Parliament.

What is important to note here is also the fact that despite the strengthening of the BJP's core Hindutva vote, the Hindutva plank alone wasn't responsible for the party's significant victories in 2014 and 2019. To put it simply, while the Hindutva appeal might be strong, it by itself is not enough to win elections—the BJP has been welfarist in its approach so as to secure votes from across the spectrum. The party has also been working towards trying to expand its influence in southern India where it has observed the adverse effects of aggressive Hindutva. In a national executive meeting, it also decided to strategize on how to bring Muslim voters on to their side, particularly targeting marginalized and poor Muslim communities. Jamal Siddiqui, the national president of the BJP minority wing, has stated in the past that they have formed a state-level team for outreach programmes among marginalized communities like the Pasmanda and Bohra Muslims. Besides, sixty-four Lok Sabha seats have been identified across the country—these are constituencies with a Muslim population of 30 per cent or more. The aim is to create 5000 Modi friends in each of these Lok Sabha constituencies.

Overall, the campaign's focus in 2024 remained on PM Modi, highlighting his welfare schemes and foreign and economic policy achievements. With these strategic manoeuvres, the BJP aimed to strengthen its position, prioritizing both fresh faces and established figures to ensure electoral success.

As the 2024 general election approached, the BJP's strategy appeared to revolve around creating a narrative pitting OBCs and Dalits against Muslims. This approach was starkly contrasted by the INDIA bloc, which emphasized safeguarding constitutional principles, while the BJP raised concerns about the endangerment of reservation policies under their government. Prime Minister Narendra Modi himself actively engaged in countering these narratives, alleging that the Opposition aimed to divert reservations meant for Dalits and backward classes to Muslims. His references to Muslims in campaign speeches ignited controversy, with opposition parties accusing him of delivering hate speeches and lodging complaints with the Election Commission.

Modi's aggressive stance on this issue marked a notable departure in electoral tactics, purportedly aimed at stemming the flow of Dalit and backward class support towards the opposition alliance. However, in a subsequent media interview, he refuted allegations of targeting Muslims in his campaign rhetoric. Despite these efforts, the BJP's attempt to paint Muslims as outliers did not yield the intended results. Instead, it inadvertently galvanized Muslim voters, who turned out in silent unity at the polls.

When the election results were announced, it became evident that the BJP's strategy had mixed outcomes. While the party maintained its hold in several regions, the broader narrative and its divisive undertones did not universally resonate as expected. This episode underscored the complex interplay of identity politics and electoral strategies in India's democratic landscape, revealing both the potential and limitations of such approaches in influencing voter behaviour and electoral outcomes.

Chapter 8

Of Ideology and Semantics;
New Parliament and New Names

Time: Sometime in May 2023

Place: Family WhatsApp group

Pijus: Congratulations to everyone on the inauguration of the new Parliament building! We must plan a trip to Delhi together to see this new symbol of national pride.

Rajshri: You echo my sentiments, Pijus. It's a matter of great pride for us that we are creating a new India.

Anindya: True, Rajshri Kakima. It was about time we got out of the shadow of our colonial past.

Atanu: The new building is cool, but somehow I do not agree with your sentiments. I mean, what is with all this renaming of

---

This WhatsApp group is demonstrative of the popular outpourings and messages that were in circulation during these events. The participants in the chat are fictional. Any similarity to actual persons, living or dead, is purely coincidental.

towns and streets in the name of creating a new India? We can put our resources to better use.

Pijus: I am surprised you are saying this. There are examples the world over of the renaming of cities. The city that was known as St Petersburg in imperial Russia was renamed Petrograd in 1914 at the start of World War I because it was felt that its original name sounded too German. Now what is wrong with that?

Anindya: Yes, that's right. In recent decades statues of communist leaders have been removed in countries that were formerly under the Soviet influence.

Rajshri: It is becoming fashionable to oppose anything that the ruling party does, and Atanu, I am sorry to say you seem to be falling into this trap too.

Atanu: Far from it. I think this isn't so much an attempt to reclaim India from its colonial past but to bolster a particular brand of Hindu nationalism. But I guess that is my opinion. To each their own!

* * *

Virasat se vikas

'In every nation's journey of development, there are moments that become immortalized forever. Some dates etch an indelible signature on the forehead of history. Today, the 29th of May 2023, is one such auspicious occasion. The country is celebrating "Amrit Mahotsav" on the occasion of seventy-five years of its independence. The people of India have presented their democracy with the gift of this new Parliament House in this Amrit Mahotsav,' PM Modi said on the inauguration of the new Parliament building.

When the new Parliament was inaugurated by Prime Minister Modi in May 2023, his impassioned speech from inside the building called it a 'temple' of the country's democracy and an 'ideal representation of both the modern and ancient'. The new Parliament building was a part of the larger Central Vista project located in what is popularly known as Lutyens' Delhi, named after its designer, the British architect Edward Lutyens. The project was meant to revamp a number of structures in the political heart of Delhi, including the residences for the prime minister and vice president, build a new Central Secretariat, convert the North and South blocks into museums, and construct ministerial offices. It also involved renovating Rajpath, now renamed Kartavya Path, a move that was hailed by many. Says Professor Kapil Kumar, 'The name Kartavya Path does not just remind ordinary people of their duty, it also reminds all bureaucrats passing through the route every day of their "kartavya" to the nation.' The project aimed not only to give old buildings a facelift but also to cement the vision of a new India emerging out of the long shadow of its colonial past. 'There was a time when India was counted among the most prosperous and splendid nations of the world,' the PM said in his inaugural speech, adding that 'hundreds of years of slavery took away this pride from us', and that it was time to reclaim it. The new Parliament building was inaugurated with the theme of '*virasat se vikas*', from heritage to progress, with the argument that it was an effort to demonstrate a 'New India', 'a country capable of maintaining its ancient heritage and restoring its spiritual and cultural glory while simultaneously making advancements towards its modern aspirations'.[1] As we sat in the press gallery during the inauguration ceremony of the Parliament building, which in the coming days would witness a new journey for Indian democracy, the prime minister explained his vision: 'Whatever stops, its destiny also stops. But what keeps moving forward, its destiny advances, touching heights. So keep moving, keep moving.'

In the preceding days, however, the inauguration of the building had become a flashpoint, with the Opposition criticizing the prime minister's decision to 'inaugurate the new parliament building by himself' as opposed to it being inaugurated by the President as head of the government and the first citizen of India.[2] While President Murmu, who did not attend the inauguration, subsequently went on to share that she was 'deeply satisfied' that Prime Minister Narendra Modi had inaugurated the new structure, and called the new building 'an important milestone in our democratic journey', the Opposition saw it as 'not only a grave insult but a direct assault on our democracy which demands a commensurate response'. A joint statement issued by nineteen national and regional opposition parties went on to state that they would collectively boycott the event, adding that 'the soul of democracy has been sucked out from the parliament'.[3]

What was also a point of criticism by the Opposition was the date that was fixed for the inauguration of the Parliament, which coincided with the birth anniversary of the RSS ideologue V.D. Savarkar, who is hailed as a hero for birthing the nationalist idea of Hindutva. Author Nilanjan Mukhopadhyay opines that the entire process, from the foundation stone that was laid for the new Parliament building in December 2020 to the meticulously chosen inauguration date coinciding with Savarkar's birth anniversary, 'was definitely not coincidental . . . There were many other days which could have been chosen but that was deliberately, possibly picked up and chosen without actually making a mention of it,' he says.

The ruling BJP, of course, went on to defend its decision by stating that the new building is a matter of pride for all Indians and accused the Opposition of 'politicizing' the inauguration. India's home minister, Amit Shah, clarified that all political parties had been invited to the ceremony, but that 'everyone will act according to their own feelings'.[4] The narrative therefore quickly changed to the Opposition's unwillingness to be a part of an India that is reclaiming its civilizational glory. The conflict was yet another reminder of the strained relationship between the governing BJP and the opposition parties.

What added to the war of words between the BJP and the Opposition, especially the Congress, was to do with the Sengol—a historical sceptre that signifies authority and power. BJP's claim was that Lord Mountbatten had presented a Sengol to Nehru when the British handed over the reins of power to the Government of India. The narrative went that Nehru had sought the counsel of Chakravarti Rajagopalachari, (the only Indian governor-general of independent India and the founder and leader of the Swatantra (Independent) Party), who had said that the reins should be handed over in the same manner as was done centuries ago by south India's Chera, Chola and Pandya dynasties. Accordingly, 'Pandit Jawaharlal Nehru accepted Sengol at around 10.45 p.m. of August 14, 1947, through the Adhinam of Tamil Nadu; it was a sign of the shift of power from Britishers to the people of our country,' Home Minister Amit Shah was quoted as saying.[5] It was this Sengol, the BJP claimed (which should have been given due respect but was kept on display as a 'walking stick' at a museum), that was being reinstated in the new Parliament building, next to the seat of the Lok Sabha Speaker. The Congress termed the entire story 'bogus' with senior leader Jairam Ramesh claiming 'lack of documented evidence'.

Coming back to the Parliament building, many thinkers agreed with the prime minister's view that it was an example of India leaving behind the mentality of slavery. They felt that it was the era of *nav jagran* or renaissance and that PM Modi and the BJP were trying to boost the self-confidence of various social communities in India. Speaking specifically of the new Parliament building, Professor Kapil Kumar highlights four important dimensions that need to be remembered. 'The first is the psychological aspect that is to do with shedding the colonial past. The old building reflected many of the atrocious decisions taken about Bharat during the British period and in a sense the new building is about shedding the Brown Sahib era. The second aspect is purely professional. The old building did not cater to the present requirements of the Parliament or Parliamentarians any longer and therefore needed to be redone. The third aspect that I want to highlight is the period in which the building was made. It was Covid time when employment was a huge issue. Don't forget even in ancient times whenever there was a famine or any natural calamity the rulers of that time used to ensure there was construction work that could provide employment to people so that they could earn their livelihood. The fourth aspect is to do with the fact that the Central Vista project, with its museums and more, will showcase the heritage and the history of India, which again will go a long way in creating a natural awakening in the country.'

Critics, however, disagree, and among other things have critiqued the price tag of the Central Vista project, especially given the fact that it was announced just prior to the Covid-19 pandemic. The Opposition claimed that the funds could have been put to better use on pandemic relief. The biggest criticism levelled against the new Parliament building, however, is that it is seen as PM Modi's attempt to not just reclaim India from its colonial past but also to bolster his own brand of Hindu nationalism. As a matter of fact, PM Modi has frequently spoken about how the Central Vista project had incorporated numerous motifs such as the peacock, the lotus flower and the banyan tree. The institutions of national pride were seen as becoming symbols of Hindu pride by many. In fact, the design of the new Parliament building also sparked debate, with some observers opining that the old structure held more aesthetic appeal. This discussion inadvertently highlighted broader concerns about balancing modernity with heritage preservation in national symbols. Among the youth, there was a notable apprehension that excessive focus on traditionalism could stifle progress and innovation.

Author Nilanjan Mukhopadhyay, for instance, sees the inauguration of the new Parliament building as a potent symbol of a larger sociopolitical trend. Sharing his insights on the trend of 'nav jagran' and the narrative of claiming and reclaiming heritage, he begins by framing the context within the broader perspective of Prime Minister Modi's tenure, noting the consistent effort to mainstream the idea of Hindu nationalism. 'Nav jagran,' he asserts, 'is just another one of those projects which have been undertaken to push a certain viewpoint, a certain ideology, mainstream it.' Author and political commentator Asim also comments on the aspect of Hindu nationalism when he says that 'the discourses and rituals surrounding the new Parliament can be seen as the rooting of popular sovereignty in the norms centred around the religious community/identity of Hindus'. He goes on to add that 'PM Modi clearly sees himself playing the part of a national redeemer with a historical zone (akin to Mao's refashioning of the power geography around Tiananmen Square). Hindu nationalism does not see the locus of ultimate sovereignty in the Parliament in an institutional sense, but locates sovereignty in the body of the Hindu people, or the Hindu nation.'

Several analysts have also pointed out that the Parliament isn't a one-off instance and that the nation has been witnessing several changes in the name of reclaiming so-called Hindu pride. Especially in his second term, it was seen that PM Modi's leadership continued to speak about freeing BJP from servitude, freeing it from sub-nationalism and re-establishing Hindu traditions and inheritance. Among other things, what has been observed are several instances of developing new sections at various religious sites in what is being positioned as 'declaring freedom from slave mentality'. 'The process of rejuvenating symbols of India that started from Somnath has now turned into a full-fledged campaign. Rejuvenation of Kashi Vishwanath Temple, Mahakal Mahalok, Kedarnath Dham and Buddha Circuit are opening the path of development and boosting economy while works on Ram Circuit would be completed soon. The world will witness the opening of Ram Mandir in Ayodhya after a few weeks only,' Prime Minister Modi was quoted as saying as he spoke at the inauguration of Swarved Mahamandir, the world's largest meditation centre.[6]

In the course of our extensive on-the-ground coverage during the Madhya Pradesh assembly elections, we witnessed a strong echo of PM Modi's thought process. Speaking to Suresh Patel, a betel vendor in Ujjain, for instance, we realized that he would vote for the BJP solely on the basis of the work done on the Mahakal Mahalok corridor near the Mahakaleshwar Temple. While he may have had complaints on other issues, he connected with the change on this one issue. Surely Suresh Patel wasn't alone and several others echoed his thoughts.

New Names

What has also been rampant is giving new names to a number of familiar landmarks. Not only were several roads named after Mughal emperors renamed, Mughal Gardens at the President of India's residence, Rashtrapati Bhavan, was renamed 'Amrit Udyan'. To be fair, this isn't really a recent trend. Since independence in 1947, several Indian governments have been known to rename cities named by the British colonists. In 1995, much before the BJP came to power, Bombay became Mumbai, Madras became Chennai (1996), Calcutta became Kolkata (2001) and Pondicherry became Puducherry (2006). Benares was changed to Varanasi as early as 1956. Critics, however, point out that post 2014, the process has been considerably accelerated and is aimed towards Hinduizing cities. Allahabad, a major Hindu pilgrimage site at the confluence of the Ganges and Yamuna rivers in Uttar Pradesh, was transformed into Prayagraj to get rid of its Islamic heritage and reconnect it with its Hindu roots. Uttar Pradesh's iconic railway station Mughalsarai Junction was formally renamed after RSS ideologue Deen Dayal Upadhyaya. Each move drew flak from the Opposition, which accused the ruling party of attempting to tamper with history. In New Delhi, when the majestic Rajpath and Central Vista lawns were renamed Kartavya Path, the government pitched it as a move to shed colonial baggage and a reminder that public service is about 'duties and not the right to rule'. However, critics point out that it is a matter of semantics, given that it was 'Kingsway' that was renamed as Rajpath in 1947, after we won freedom. Another thoroughfare that intersected it, 'Queensway', was similarly renamed Janpath, or the people's way. Both were assertions of Indian sovereignty and thus another renaming was unnecessary.

While defenders say India is simply reclaiming its history, critics worry that all of this is an example of an exclusionary mindset. Noted historian, Irfan, points out how Swami Vivekananda serves as a beacon of true enlightenment, celebrating Muslim history and Mughal architecture. 'Yet, the contemporary push for a new awakening involves the removal of symbols from the Mughal era, seeking a fresh start,' he laments. 'This rejuvenation should steer clear of discrimination and negativity. In today's context, political agendas often overshadow genuine social harmony,' he opines.

'India That Is Bharat'

What has also been widely debated is the likelihood of changing the country's name from India to Bharat. The debate gained momentum during the G20 Summit in September 2023 around a dinner honouring the participating heads of state. The invites referred to the President of India, Droupadi Murmu, as 'President of Bharat', a move that sparked controversy. It didn't help that the news of the invites came two days after Mohan Bhagwat, the chief of the RSS, an ideological mentor of the BJP, said in a speech that the country should use the word Bharat instead of India. 'At times we use India so those who speak English will understand. But we must stop using this. The name of the country Bharat will remain Bharat wherever you go in the world,' Bhagwat had said.[7]

Since then, the term 'Bharat' has been increasingly used instead of 'India' by the government. Several people came out in support of the nomenclature. Former Indian cricketer Virender Sehwag was among the many who put out a public post stating: 'I have always believed a name should be one which instils pride in us. We are Bhartiyas, India is a name given by the British and it has been long overdue to get our original name "Bharat" back officially.'[8] Several others praised the potential change as being authentic to India's history. Critics, however, saw its use as the latest sign of a nationalist push. Amidst legal and constitutional experts clarifying that there was no illegality in the use of 'Bharat' in place of 'India' in any official communication as it was part of the Constitution, which reads 'India, that is Bharat', it remained uncertain if the Centre would formally propose renaming the country Bharat.

Pedagogy or Propaganda

'Nobody can stop us from writing history as we are independent now,' declared Union Home Minister Amit Shah.[9]

The theme of reclaiming Hindu pride was also being witnessed in changes being made to history books. Shah was quoted as saying that our history books are disproportionately focused on the exploits of the Mughals and didn't give due credit to such great dynasties as the Mauryas, Guptas, Pandyas, Cholas and so on. The theme of reviving the glory of the past for the present was seen in school textbooks being edited to drop chapters on the history of Mughal courts, the Naxalite movement and the mention of Dalit writers.[10]

Supporters of the exercise argued that some degree of course correction in school history textbooks was necessary because these books gave too much importance to Mughal rulers. Others, however, say this is akin to presenting an oversimplified version of India's syncretic past. Changes made in textbooks also led up to 250 historians from leading Indian and foreign universities across India issuing a public statement as they felt that the selective deletion in textbook revision reflected the sway of divisive politics over pedagogical concerns. 'The chapters deleted from the history textbook are precisely those which do not fit into the pseudo-historical schema of the ruling dispensation. Excising any period from the study of the past would make students unable to comprehend the connecting thread of the past with the present times, and would deprive students of an opportunity to connect, compare and contrast the past and the present, and would disrupt the organic interconnectedness of the subject-matter of the discipline,' the statement read.[11]

While the National Council of Educational Research and Training (NCERT) went on to clarify that the changes, which were first announced as part of a syllabus 'rationalization' exercise, wouldn't affect knowledge but instead reduce the load on children after the Covid-19 pandemic, critics felt that the omissions were worrying and would affect the students' understanding of their country. 'What is happening now is a suggestion that the Mughals were peculiarly violent—when in fact violence was part of kingship as an institution everywhere—and that they saw themselves primarily as Muslims, determined to torment Hindus,' historian and author Manu S. Pillai was quoted as saying.[12]

While critics level charges of the saffronization of education, the ruling dispensation calls it a shedding of the colonial mindset and taking pride in one's Indian identity. Former vice president M. Venkaiah Naidu, in his address after inaugurating the South Asian Institute of Peace and Reconciliation, had asked, 'what is wrong with saffron' as he called for a total rejection of the Macaulay system of education in the country.

All the World's a Stage

While attempts were being made to preserve India's heritage nationally, PM Modi also tried to showcase India's rich heritage on the world stage. When he met American President Biden and his wife in June 2023, he took special gifts from India for them. Among other things was a unique sandalwood box sourced from Mysore. The box contained an idol of Lord Ganesha, the Hindu deity considered to be the destroyer of obstacles. With President Biden reaching the milestone of eighty years and eight months, a press note made a mention of the fact that it was an important milestone in the Hindu way of life as ancient Indian texts mention that an individual becomes '*drishta sahasrachandro*', or one who has seen a thousand full moons, when he completes the age of eighty years and eight months. President Biden was also presented with a copy of the first English translation of the book *The Ten Principal Upanishads*. It helped that the authors were Biden's favourite poet, William Butler Yeats, and Shri Purohit Swami.[13]

Uttar Pradesh Chief Minister Yogi Adityanath, on an earlier occasion, was quoted as saying that previously, gifts given to foreign dignitaries 'were Agra's Taj Mahal or some *minar* that has no connection with India's culture or heritage . . . This is the first time this has happened that when India's prime minister Narendra Modi goes abroad, or any foreign president visits India, he is gifted the Shrimad Bhagavad Gita or Ramayan.'[14]

Even though PM Modi's gifts to foreign dignitaries have comprised more than religious books, critics point out that all of this is indicative of strong tendencies to saffronize India's foreign policy.

Sweet Spot

While attacks by the Opposition and rebuttals by the dispensation have become par for the course in this reclamation of identity battle, an observation by social expert and psephologist, Yashwant Deshmukh, highlights the correlation between economic prosperity, the rise of the middle class and the rekindling of Hindu identity. 'This nexus', according to Deshmukh, 'has been tactfully utilized by political entities like the BJP, particularly under Narendra Modi's leadership, to awaken and appease the sense of Hindu pride and belonging through various schemes and actions.' He suggests that while these sentiments are effectively harnessed by political parties in power, this resurgence is not a permanent phenomenon. 'It seems to be contingent upon the satisfaction and smooth livelihoods of this middle-class segment. When their daily lives remain untroubled and content, their attention is directed towards these narratives. However, if faced with significant challenges or disruptions, their focus would shift away from these socio-political ideals,' he opines. Deshmukh seems to imply that these identitarian and political movements thrive in an environment of stability and prosperity. 'The attention towards reclaiming heritage and strengthening cultural identity appears to be a response to economic stability, accentuated during the years following 2014, rather than a cause in itself,' he says.

Other political analysts have also referred to a similar sweet spot that we are in at the moment with the rise of the aspirational middle class.

As things stand, the debate between reclaiming India from its colonial past versus bolstering Hindu nationalism will continue to rage.

Overall, while the BJP continues to emphasize evoking a sense of resurgence of a Golden Age, these efforts sometimes appeared excessive and overshadow critical issues like developmental legacy.

During the Bharat Jodo Yatra, Rahul Gandhi consistently raised concerns about these issues, suggesting that the government's policies were neglecting contemporary challenges. Opposition parties seized upon these sentiments during General Elections, particularly emphasizing the exclusion of marginalized communities from the narrative of heritage preservation. This discourse illustrated a larger struggle within Indian politics to reconcile historical pride with the imperatives of a rapidly changing society.

Chapter 9

Popular Culture: The New Battleground

Time: Sometime in 2022

Place: WhatsApp group of Gen Z friends from school

Vikas: Film Recommendation Alert! You guys must watch *The Kashmir Files*. The film has dared to show the truth that was so long suppressed.

Reyansh: I watched it last night too. Truly, we have been insensitive towards the suffering of Kashmiri Pandits.

Atishi: True dat. It was heart-wrenching to watch the exodus of Kashmiri Pandits from the Valley at the height of militancy in the '90s.

Saket: Not sure why you guys are lauding the film. It is sheer propaganda. They are simply peddling hate.

This WhatsApp group is demonstrative of the popular outpourings and messages that were in circulation during these events. The participants in the chat are fictional. Any similarity to actual persons, living or dead, is purely coincidental.

Vikas: This is like calling *Schindler's List* a propaganda film. It's high time we stepped out of denial and looked facts in the eye.

Reyansh: I agree. The film needs to be watched by a maximum number of people. I must confess that I wasn't aware of the pain, suffering, struggle and trauma faced by Kashmiri Hindus in the '90s.

Saket: I strongly believe that the film has twisted and distorted history simply to whip up anger and incite hate. The ruling dispensation has smartly bolstered majoritarian cinema; almost as if cinema has emerged as the new spokesperson of Hindutva politics. This is simply a divide-and-rule strategy.

Atishi: No matter how much you deny it, the truth will eventually prevail.

* * *

'How's the Josh?'

Cinema and politics have been intertwined in India from time immemorial. From Indian movies depicting social and political concerns in their plot lines to actors turning to politics post their film careers, the impact of politics on cinema in particular and popular culture in general, has been all-encompassing.

In recent years cinema has been particularly emerging as a battleground for shaping public opinion and national identity. Take the instance of films such as *Toilet: Ek Prem Katha*, which promoted the Swachh Bharat Mission, or *Commando 2*, which delineated the benefits of demonetization, or *Uri: The Surgical Strike*, which had the public celebrating military action; all of these films have showcased the huge impact of political cinema on the public. Then there has been a string of political biopics, such as the one on PM Modi, another on Bal Thackeray, both of which lionized their subjects, while the one on Dr Manmohan Singh mocked him and the Congress.

'It's not the first time we're witnessing such a cultural shift,' says film director, Avinash Das. 'Post-independence, filmmakers like Guru Dutt, Bimal Roy and Raj Kapoor portrayed the tales of joys and sorrows of that era. Characters in cinema during that time reflected the circumstances of that period. Around the Emergency, Amitabh Bachchan emerged as an angry young man, connecting society to the frustration of the youth. Subsequently, cinema of the 1980s highlighted society's injustices and complexities with a touch of lowliness. After Rajiv Gandhi's era of liberalization, cinema began selling dreams of transforming India into Switzerland. Similarly, today's cinema reflects the turmoil of the times. Cinema, being an artistic tool influenced by capitalist structures, cannot remain entirely independent. Every era comes with its impact, and in that culture, many seek to maximize their gains by immersing themselves.' Film scholar Ashish Rajadhyaksha, in his book *Indian Cinema: A Very Short Introduction* (Oxford: Oxford University Press, 2016), similarly directs us to Shyam Benegal's new cinema that comprised films such as *Manthan*, which was based on milk cooperatives in Gujarat, *Arohan*, based on the land redistribution programme of a leftist government in West Bengal, *Susman* on handloom cooperatives, *Yatra* on Indian Railways and so on.

In recent times, however, the relationship between the rise of ethnic majoritarianism in India and the role of the Mumbai film industry in it has been hotly debated. One film that particularly became a lightning rod for debates on the portrayal of historical events in popular culture was *The Kashmir Files*. Directed by Vivek Agnihotri, the film claimed to shed light on the exodus of Kashmiri Pandits from the Valley during the early 1990s. The film became one of the biggest grossers. Made on a budget of just Rs 15 crore, *The Kashmir Files* raked in over Rs 350 crore at the box office, and that too, without any big stars. It helped that the mainstream entertainment media did not have many films based on the Kashmir issue—a previous film on the issue, *Shikara* by Vidhu Vinod Chopra, had been criticized for being too weak and diluted. While some lauded *The Kashmir Files* as a well-made film, many others credited its success to its marketing. Whirlwind discussions about it on 24x7 news channels as well as social media forwards helped its cause. It also helped that the movie went on to receive support from several BJP-ruled states, with tax-free status accorded to it, besides winning a ringing endorsement from the prime minister of the country. '*The Kashmir Files* is a very good movie. All of you should watch it. More such movies should be made,' PM Modi was quoted as saying to his party colleagues gathered for a BJP parliamentary meeting.[1]

The movie's director, Vivek Agnihotri, decoded the film's commercial success as the younger generation's demand for 'facts'. 'It was not that Kashmir was not reported, but that Kashmir was reported half-heartedly in the media. Someone killed in Kashmir, people would find it on the sixth or seventh page of the newspaper. It was never a subject of prime-time discussion, unless something major like the Balakot incident happened,' Agnihotri says by way of explanation. Another aspect that he thinks was responsible for the success of the movie was that ever since Article 370 was abrogated in 2019 (which granted special status to Jammu and Kashmir), Kashmir had been in the news. 'The younger generation could not comprehend jargon like "abrogation" or "Article 370". They couldn't understand these technicalities,' he points out. 'In fact, two generations accepted the film—those who were born in the

70s and 80s, and the new generation. People born in the 70s and early 80s had some idea (about Kashmir) and they were frustrated because every time the narrative that was presented was that Kashmir has been illegally occupied by India and they knew that wasn't true. And the new generation, they did not know why the Kashmiri Pandits don't exist in Kashmir. *The Kashmir Files* addressed that in a very unapologetic manner and it was based on the interviews of the real victims and therefore the credibility and authenticity of the reporting . . . I think that's why people accepted it,' Agnihotri says.

Enumerating the many reasons for its blockbuster success, Agnihotri further explains, '*The Kashmir Files* disrupted the cinematic market . . . Audiences, tired of formulaic Westernized narratives, find solace in stories grounded in their cultural reality . . . When films like *Kashmir Files* come, then suddenly people say "Aha, this is also an option we can go to the theatre and watch and we don't have to watch all these La La Land, NRI-catering kind of cinema" . . . The foundation of India's roots is in nationalism. That is why you will find that nationalism is something which can never die in this country.'

Not everyone agrees with Agnihotri's reasoning. Critics argued that the film presented a narrative that was overtly one-sided and that the film contributed to the polarization of public opinion by presenting a selective interpretation of historical events. It was also pointed out that cinematic narratives of hyper-nationalism, toxic masculinity and divisive propagandist politics were finding favour with the audiences.

In fact, critics cited dialogues from the film *Uri* as an example of this kind of 'guts-and-glory' propaganda:

Yeh naya Hindustan hai, yeh ghar mein ghusega bhi, aur marega bhi (This is a new India, it will infiltrate the house, as well as slay inside).

Waqt aa gaya hai, khoon ka badla khoon se lene ka (It is time to take revenge with blood).

A year after *The Kashmir Files*, Sudipto Sen's *The Kerala Story* hit the silver screen with similar aplomb. In this case, the trailer itself triggered a row, claiming that around 32,000 women from the state were 'converted' to Islam and recruited by the Islamic State (IS). The trailer went on to show a Muslim cleric advising some young men to entrap Hindu and Christian women, and impregnate them if required, only to convert them to Islam and send them to west Asian countries to join the terrorist group IS. A young woman in police custody was seen offering to tell the cops the history behind her entry into terrorism, while a hijab-clad young woman was seen convincing a friend that wearing a hijab protects her from sexual assault.

There were immediate calls for banning the movie, with several Kerala politicians alleging that the movie was an attempt to tarnish the state's image and to spread hatred among people. Chief Minister Pinarayi Vijayan termed the movie a 'Sangh Parivar propaganda' piece.[2]

The BJP's national IT cell chief Amit Malviya, on the other hand, described the film as 'based on real-life stories' which were 'shocking and disturbing'. 'The movie portrays the rapid Islamisation of Kerala and how innocent girls are being trapped and groomed to be used as cannon fodder for ISIS. Love Jihad is real and dangerous,' he tweeted.[3]

Our interview with the film's producer Vipul Amrutlal Shah saw him addressing the issue of the film being branded as 'propaganda' head-on. 'The film was portraying an uncomfortable truth and when 'people cannot challenge the truth, they then label it as propaganda,' he asserted. 'Political ideology,' he went on to explain, 'was always part of Hindi cinema. When *Manthan* was made or *Godan* was made they were not labelled as left-wing cinema or whatever. I think social media is playing a very important role in labelling films, and because of that a lot more new audiences have started coming to cinema halls.'

Film critic Mayank Shekhar adds yet another interesting aspect to the discussion on propaganda versus art, when he clarifies that 'propaganda is, after all, a legit genre, whether in literature, journalism, indeed, in films and television. And I don't mean this as a pejorative—simply as a description of it.' He goes on to add that the 'purpose of propaganda is also to consciously select which events to highlight, and which to altogether omit. Therefore their degrees may vary, but *The Kashmir Files*, *The Kerala Story*, *The Accidental Prime Minister*, or for that matter, *Main Atal Hoon* (a biopic on the late prime minister Atal Bihari Vajpayee) are all political propaganda films.' Ask him if there has been an upward swing in this genre and his answer is an unequivocal 'yes'. 'You sense it more and more in the portrayal of patriotism veering towards jingoism, in particular, which as a phenomenon, isn't limited to popular Indian cinema,' he adds. He, however, goes on to clarify that there isn't necessarily a positive correlation between political propaganda films and their box office success or viewership on the smaller screen. 'I suspect people watch movies for multiple reasons—stories, trailer, reviews, performances, cast, craft, locations, etc., etc. Simply a film hammering in a political agenda can't guarantee entertainment, the primary purpose of movies,' he explains. Even though he does agree there could be exceptions. He goes on to add that 'pop culture can't help but reflect its times. Only that we can best make sense of its output in hindsight. So the 70s, anti-establishment, "angry young man" films of Salim-Javed may be perceived as depicting the frustration of the unemployed young in that decade—the loss of India's founding fathers' dreams, as it were. But while they were being made, they were really the action films of those times! Also, you can't predict artistic responses.' Excessive censorship, he feels, 'gives birth to subtle, art-house Iranian cinema, full of metaphors, or can result in the throttled Chinese entertainment that is soft-power nowhere in the world!'

Coming back to *The Kerala Story* in particular, Sudipto Sen, the film's director, was quoted as saying that 'We expected it to be a hit, though maybe not this big. We knew the subject would touch the right chord.'[4] In fact, in the face of the success enjoyed by both *The Kashmir Files* and *The Kerala Story*, such movies became the flavour of the season. Agnihotri, for instance, went on to work on *The Vaccine Story*, which aimed to tell the inside story of Indian vaccinologists and scientists who battled Covid-19. The film, however, bombed at the box office, proving that the narrative of nationalism doesn't necessarily mean commercial success.

Veteran film-maker Sudhir Mishra has a different view on why movies such as *The Kashmir Files* and *The Kerala Story* became popular. He feels that their success can be attributed to the fact that 'the movie audience comes from the same society that holds extreme views and divisiveness. Market forces now determine everything. And what influences market forces is not something innocent,' he says with a sense of finality. Touching on the subject of audience responsibility, he points out how 'you have a section of people who say they want so-and-so kind of movie, who ask "why such movies are not made", but they don't go and watch those movies in theatres. As an audience, you have to intervene at some point,' he goes on to explain. Mishra cites an example—the stark contrast between the stature of a film-maker like Anurag Kashyap at events like Jashn-e-Rekhta, the world's largest Urdu language literary festival, and the actual viewership of his films. 'You can see Kashyap's stardom at events like Rekhta, but then people don't go and watch his movies like *Almost Pyaar with DJ Mohabbat*. Then what is the point?' questions Mishra, pointing to the challenge of translating critical acclaim into box office success.

He, however, vehemently opposes calls for bans against any movie. 'You may not like a movie like *Animal*, for instance, but you cannot ask such movies to be stopped being shown. An answer to one movie can only be another movie,' Mishra stresses.

Interestingly, Mishra's call for the 'answer to one movie being another movie' is being answered not just by cinema but also by the comedic and digital realms, which are fast emerging as counter narratives.

Comedy as Resistance

At one time the realm of humour was limited to the silver screen, and it carried its own unique charm. It was in the 1950s that the comedic spotlight shone on the common man's struggles, epitomized by Johnny Walker's timeless tunes like *Sar jo tera chakraye*. From Bollywood to sarcastic TV gems like *Sarabhai vs Sarabhai* and *Khichdi*, the baton was slowly but surely passed to the era of stand-up comedy. In a notable cultural shift, the over-the-top (OTT) platforms have also brought with them a wave of diverse content challenging traditional norms and pushing boundaries, while stand-up comedians use humour as a tool to dissect and question narratives.

As the laughter landscape evolves, however, the fine line between comedy and controversy continues to become blurrier. The uproar surrounding Tanmay Bhat's Snapchat video, poking fun at Lata Mangeshkar and Sachin Tendulkar, for instance, echoed the changing dynamics. Such controversies, of course, are not new—Kiku Sharda's arrest after he mimicked Baba Gurmeet Ram Rahim Singh, Kapil Sharma's run-in with nurses in Amritsar protesting his allegedly 'vulgar' portrayal of the nursing profession, and the infamous AIB controversy, which unlocked locker room humour and uploaded it as a performance and landed Karan Johar, Ranveer Singh and Arjun Kapoor in hot water, are some of the more popular examples.

Comedians like Vir Das, Kunal Kamra, Varun Grover and several others have also made news for their political comedy and have equally been called out for hurting sentiments. Kamra wrote a lengthy Facebook post that went viral, addressing the fallout of being political and outspoken: among them, eviction, rejection and last-minute cancellations. 'We Indians have a world record in getting our feelings hurt,'[5] he was quoted as saying. But even as Kamra lamented the shrinking of freedoms in India, he remained defiant. Fear, Kamra felt, was today an 'undercurrent' that flowed through the subconscious minds of all stand-up comics. 'If you arrest someone or file a case against them, you don't need to use additional force. The comedian will immediately do what is correct for them and their family,' Kamra was quoted to have said. Speaking of arrests, comedian Munawar Faruqui was arrested based on the allegation that his jokes had insulted Hindu deities. The case was filed based on a complaint by the convenor of the Hindu Rakshak Sangathan and was initially heard by the Madhya Pradesh High Court, which declined him bail saying, 'liberty of a person has to be balanced with his duties towards other citizens'.[6] Faruqui was subsequently granted interim bail by the Supreme Court more than a month after he was arrested.

Vir Das, the famous stand-up comic, similarly ran into trouble when he ended his November 2021 performance at the Kennedy Center in Washington, DC, by reciting his poem 'I come from two Indias': 'I come from an India where we worship women during the day and gang-rape them at night' went his piece. The backlash was swift.[7] Aditya Jha, a spokesperson of the BJP, filed a police complaint against Das accusing him of making 'derogatory statements against women and India' and called for his immediate arrest. Das also faced criticism from some fellow performers, including actress Kangana Ranaut who called his actions 'soft terrorism' in an Instagram story, adding that 'strict action should be taken against such criminals'.[8] However, several opposition politicians stood up for the comedian. Writing on Twitter, Shashi Tharoor, a member of the Congress Party, said Das 'spoke for millions' besides calling him a 'stand-up comedian who knows the real meaning of the term "stand up" is not physical but moral'.

Amidst the backlash, Das issued a statement saying his intention was to remind everyone that India, despite its issues, was 'great'. 'The video is a satire about the duality of two very separate Indias that do different things. Like any nation, it has light and dark, good and evil within it. None of this is a secret. The video appeals to us to never forget that we are great. To never stop focusing on what makes us great,' his statement read.[9] 'I don't think laughter is a threat,' he was quoted as saying in a statement to America's National Public Radio (NPR).

Neeti Palta, another popular stand-up comedian, is of the opinion that political humour is not taken lightly in India. 'You know what does it take to be a stand-up comedian?' she asks. 'Quick wit, quicker legs and a lawyer on speed dial,'[10] is her reply.

Those challenges apart, stand-up comedians continue to act as the voice of the anti-establishment sentiment in some measure, driven in part by mainstream media's pro-government stance. Shyam Rangeela, for instance, who gained recognition through his mimicry and satire of Narendra Modi, even went as far as attempting to symbolically contest the elections against him from the Varanasi Lok Sabha seat in Uttar Pradesh. His nomination, however, was rejected.

If you think comedy could and should achieve much more in the political arena, you need to hear this interesting story narrated by social expert and psephologist, Yashwant Deshmukh, 'Years ago Gulzar was asked why you don't make comedy films like *Angoor* any more.' As an answer to this question, Gulzar explained that 'comedy films can be successful in two types of societies. One, which is extremely prosperous, which can laugh at itself. The other, which is completely ruined, which has nothing to lose.' Because Indian society is neither extremely prosperous nor completely ruined, things like comedy do not work here, he believed.

That said, the influence of popular culture on art is growing. Recent times, among other things, have seen new musical groups and bands who often use the power of music to share their thoughts about society. In Punjab, for instance, there was the rise of the sub-genre of political music that calls itself Chamar Rap/Chamar Pop, which asks the Dalit community to unify against forces of social inequity and economic deprivation. While the art and music movement to do with Dalit resistance began years ago, the rise of Dalit singers like Ginni Mahi took the modern Ambedkarite assertion of equal rights one step ahead. A young female voice dominating a primarily male musical tradition only reiterated the possibilities of protest music. Similarly, amidst protests against the CAA-National Register of Citizens (NRC) laws, Faiz Ahmed Faiz's poetry was continuously heard. Verses by poet-songwriters like Aamir Aziz and Varun Grover, to name a few, also resonated across anti-CAA protest sites. Similarly, when parts of India erupted in anger against the three new farm laws, *Farmers Rap* made its appearance as a voice of dissent against them. It is clear that India is witnessing a revival of protest music with the genre throwing up new voices and fresh perspectives with passionate takes on burning issues. The use of music to highlight social issues isn't just true of protests, though. Ahead of the recent consecration of the Ram Temple, the country witnessed a series of musical videos of popular Ram bhajans that gained immense popularity. Singers Jubin Nautiyal and Payal Dev's devotional song *'Mere ghar Ram aaye hain'*, penned by Manoj Muntashir, for instance, became immensely popular ahead of the grand Ram Temple opening on 22 January 2024. Similarly, singers such as Swati Mishra became an overnight sensation as *'Ram ayenge'* became a popular anthem. If the historic town of Ayodhya witnessed a remarkable transformation on the consecration day of the Ram Temple, creating a spectacle that left both residents and visitors in awe, so did the music industry, with devotional songs getting a huge boost on YouTube.

Majoritarian Art vs Art as Dissent

As commercial Indian cinema and other art forms level up their political ante, some see it as a traditional case of art imitating life while others view it as the propaganda wheels being put into motion. Observers have, however, noticed a shift in mood as 2024 drew near. Films centred on prominent figures of the right-wing ideology, such as Savarkar, for instance, struggled to find traction with audiences, leading to a decline in the production of such movies. Observers pointed out that in a deeply polarized society, individuals associated with mainstream popular culture appeared increasingly defensive. They focused therefore on maintaining political correctness and avoided delving into contentious issues.

Popular culture, however, is known to operate in cycles, where trends come and go. Whether or not there is a diminishing appeal in creating films that cater to nationalist and Hindutva sentiments only time and audience tastes will tell.

Chapter 10

Boycott Culture: The Beginning of the End?

Time: Sometime in 2023

Place: Family WhatsApp group

Uncle Ashok: What's with these foreign brands? Just imagine the temerity of Starbucks, running an ad that is against Indian culture.

Aunt Reema: What ad are you talking about? I haven't seen it.

Uncle Ashok: Well, Didi, it is one of those woke ads showing a trans woman and how her family is accepting her.

Aunt Reema: Oh Lord! They are really spoiling our youth. They seriously need to be boycotted.

Isha: Don't worry, Bua, there is a full boycott gang at work. Honestly, I am amazed to see this so-called outrage and culture spiel.

This WhatsApp group is demonstrative of the popular outpourings and messages that were in circulation during these events. The participants in the chat are fictional. Any similarity to actual persons, living or dead, is purely coincidental.

Akash: You bet, Isha. This is when there are so many dastardly acts playing out in real life. And here we are protesting against these ads.

Uncle Ashok: You children do not realize that ads such as these can corrupt an entire generation.

Isha: I do not agree, Uncle. Besides, what I do not understand is why has social media become a moral arbiter of society?

Akash: Yes, and these brands, a whiff of protest and they have a knee-jerk reaction and withdraw ads.

Aunt Reema: This is the exact point Ashok and I are making. See how all these ads are corrupting the youth. You do not even have respect for the views of your elders any more.

Uncle Ashok: These children, I tell you!

* * *

The Anatomy of Boycott

'As we welcome the festival of love and light, Jashn-e-Riwaaz by Fabindia is a collection that beautifully pays homage to Indian culture.'

What would normally be considered a regular festive promotional campaign turned into a PR nightmare for clothing brand Fabindia in 2021. Their fault? Terming Diwali 'Jashn-e-Riwaaz'. It was not long before #BoycottFabindia started trending. Fabindia ended up withdrawing the said advertisement.

A year before, Indian jewellery brand Tanishq had faced a similar fate. An advertisement that depicted the baby shower of a Hindu woman married into a Muslim family met with immense hate online. Ironically, the jewellery line being advertised, titled Ekatvam (unity or oneness with divine consciousness), was accused of promoting 'love jihad' and interfaith marriage.

Online matrimony service Bharat Matrimony similarly found itself in the throes of a PR nightmare when its advertisement highlighting safety issues for women during Holi came under fire for being 'Hindu phobic'.

Other examples abound. A karwa chauth advert by Dabur featuring a same-sex couple, Surf Excel's '*daag achhe hai* (stains are good)' ad showing Hindu–Muslim unity, CEAT tyre commercial featuring Aamir Khan where the actor is seen advising people not to burn crackers on the road, have all gone through the same cycle: the advertisement is released, backlash follows on social media, there is a call for boycott of the brand, which is followed by the withdrawal of the said advertisement.

The idea of 'boycott' originated in Ireland in the 1880s. Legend has it that peasants and farmers rose in protest against Charles Cunningham Boycott, a despotic British land tax collector. The eponymous 'boycott' has since been used the world over as a method of protest.

Contemporary India has witnessed a huge surge in the boycott culture, with people increasingly resorting to calls for censorship and boycotts against advertisements, movies and products. From advertisements deemed offensive, to movies facing backlash for their content, citizens are quick to mobilize online campaigns calling for the boycott of anything perceived to be against their cultural, religious or national values. Things have come to such a pass that boycott, besides being a tool of protest, has also become a tool of intolerance and bullying with 'boycott armies' being on a rampage on social media. So much so that the spate of boycotts and cancel calls has raised concerns about the impact on creative freedom in India. Film-makers, advertisers and product manufacturers now find themselves navigating a delicate balance between artistic expression and the fear of backlash. That they are being forced to re-evaluate their content and marketing strategies is a clear reflection of the shift in power dynamics from traditional gatekeepers to the digital masses.

Social media's boycott obsession, however, isn't limited to adverts. In fact, Bollywood, which was earlier only the target of trolls and memes, has also been in the line of fire. Observers point out that the turning point came with the untimely demise of film actor Sushant Singh Rajput. Film-maker Madhur Bhandarkar was quoted as saying in a podcast, 'I have noticed that this [boycott] happened largely after the passing of Sushant Singh Rajput. Maybe the industry ignored him.'[1] Rajput's death led to netizens slamming seasoned film-makers for breeding nepotism in the industry. While the core concern of Sushant's unexplained death was put on the back-burner after a while, the unprecedented hatred against Bollywood continued to run amok.

Since then, a number of films have faced threats of a boycott, albeit for different reasons. Veteran film-maker Sudhir Mishra points out that people are becoming too sensitive. 'You can have some objection to something, but you cannot shut it down. If you don't like someone, suddenly there is an FIR against them. This will lead to creation of an atmosphere where the youth of today will be wary of speaking or even thinking.'

Examples abound. For instance, the Aamir Khan and Kareena Kapoor starrer *Laal Singh Chaddha* became the centre of controversy in 2022. Ironically, the reason for the proposed boycott was an interview given by Khan years ago, in which he had spoken about the 'growing intolerance' in India. Several boycott calls have similarly followed a very twisted and hard-to-explain-rationally logic. When *Laal Singh Chaddha* failed to make a mark at the box office, film trade analyst Taran Adarsh had tweeted, 'STOP being in denial about #Boycott calls not affecting film biz . . . The fact is, these #Boycott calls HAVE made a dent and impacted the #BO numbers of #LaalSinghChaddha specifically . . . Face it!'[2]

Observers have pointed out that when the boycott of an actor extends to the boycott of his or her movie, what is overlooked is the fact that there were hundreds of others who poured their blood, sweat and tears into its making.

That said, boycott calls do not always work out as intended. Sometimes, a boycott call can produce the opposite result. Shah Rukh Khan starrer *Pathaan* makes for an excellent case study. In January 2023, when the superstar of Bollywood, Shah Rukh Khan, was returning to the big screen after several years with *Pathaan*, the film ran into a huge controversy with things taking on a nationalistic and religious hue. Deepika Padukone's saffron-coloured bikini in the song *Besharam rang* was at the centre of a huge furore. Not only did it lead to a strong boycott call for the movie, the call also had political undertones, with the leaders of the ruling BJP party supporting the boycott appeal. In Madhya Pradesh, former home minister Narottam Mishra was among the many leaders of the ruling BJP who were seen to be openly endorsing the boycott. So much so that the party leadership had to intervene, with PM Modi advising party leaders to refrain from making 'unnecessary statements' about films.[3]

While Shah Rukh Khan remained silent throughout the controversy, the advance booking of the movie, however, did all the talking. The film's success was thunderous and felt like a vengeful response to the boycott Bollywood gang.

In an article published by the *Guardian*, Namrata Joshi, an Indian film critic and author, argued, 'There's been so much hatred pouring out on to Bollywood for the past two years, all these unsubstantiated allegations that the industry and those in it are morally questionable. The polarisation and divisions growing in our society have seeped into Bollywood, which has never happened before.' She added, 'But I think the success of *Pathaan* shows that audiences don't necessarily buy into these vindictive narratives.'[4]

Importantly, the curious case of *Laal Singh Chadha* on the one hand and *Pathaan* on the other demonstrates that there isn't a set formula for how movies facing boycott calls fare at the box office. If anything, *Pathaan* went on to demonstrate the flip side of the boycott phenomena. Critics point out that on the other hand, there are examples of movies that had all the requisite elements to attract a Hindu nationalist audience, but which tanked. Notable among them is the Akshay Kumar starrer *Samrat Prithviraj*, which eulogized a Hindu emperor. Another curious case of the boycott saga unfolded with the release of *Adipurush*. Expectations were high for a film based on mythological stories, hoping it would be liked by the Hindu audience. Amidst aggressive promotion of the film, however, a range of controversies reared their heads. Audiences were outraged by some of the movie dialogues written by Manoj Muntashir, who has spoken and written about Hindutva in recent years. The film did not go on to perform well at the box office.

That brings us to the important issue of who is really perpetrating these boycotts? While the right wing has often been the prime accused, the fact also remains that in the present age of digital activism, social media platforms such as Twitter, Instagram and Facebook have emerged as powerful tools for any and everyone to express 'opinions' and rally support.

In fact, a recent report released by the International Labour Organization stated, 'The total global number of unemployed youth is estimated to reach 73 million in 2022, a slight improvement from 2021 (75 million), but still six million above the pre-pandemic level of 2019.'[5] Observers point out that it is the trigger-happy unemployed youth who could well be honing in on trivial issues and exaggerating them.

Film-maker Vivek Agnihotri, however, reminds us that while lately there has been a lot of talk about films being subject to a digitally vocal majority that is stifling creative expression, boycott and censorship calls are not new to Indian cinema. He points out that the roots of boycott culture run deep into the annals of post-Independence India, well before the perceived surge after 2014. 'A narrative has been created that this boycott culture and censorship, all of this [has] started now, after 2014. I don't think so. Maybe it's a coincidence that social media also grew in India around the same time, that's why it is out in the open and more visible. But, we have had this culture since Independence,' Agnihotri says.

Drawing attention to historical instances, Agnihotri sheds light on the fact that figures like Majrooh Sultanpuri faced not just boycott but even arrest. Icons of Indian cinema such as Lata Mangeshkar, Kishore Kumar, Amitabh Bachchan and Dev Anand also found themselves in the cross hairs of state-sponsored boycotts. Beyond the realm of cinema, artists like M.F. Husain and contentious works like Salman Rushdie's *Satanic Verses* have also been subject to societal prohibition and boycott, Agnihotri contends.

In a historical context, parallels can be drawn with the censorship challenges faced during the Emergency period, he adds. Agnihotri points out that one only has to look at the ban on films like *Kissa Kursi Ka* and *Aandhi* to understand that political pressure has long influenced Bollywood. *Kissa Kursi*

Ka had faced allegations of mocking Sanjay Gandhi's auto-manufacturing plans. Supporters of Sanjay Gandhi took the drastic step of burning the film's master prints. Later, the film was remade with a different cast. Sanjeev Kumar and Suchitra Sen's film *Aandhi* was similarly banned during the Emergency as it was accused of inaccurately portraying Indira Gandhi's life. So, what is different about the boycott challenge that Bollywood is facing right now? 'The problem is "my boycott is better than your boycott" is now trending because of social media. People are so angry they want to outrage, people want to destroy someone,' Agnihotri adds.

Delving into the recent backlash against Bollywood, Agnihotri provides another unique perspective. He attributes the outrage during the Covid-19 pandemic to a sense of disconnection between the suffering masses and Bollywood's elite. As people grappled with the harsh realities of the pandemic, Bollywood stars were seemingly flaunting their extravagant lifestyles on social media. The stark contrast between the hardships faced by the middle class and the perceived indifference of Bollywood fuelled public anger, Agnihotri believes. He posits that the political dimension entered the narrative when politicians capitalized on this discontent, turning it into a larger, more political movement. 'That's why we feel that it's only recently that we have started boycotting Bollywood, but Bollywood has always been boycotted by political parties, by social groups, by religious groups,' *The Kashmir Files* director says.

Film-maker Avinash Das expresses a similar point of view. 'The boycott culture is not a spontaneous phenomenon; it operates under the influence of government propaganda,' he points out. 'During the Emergency, political films like *Kissa Kursi Ka* were censored. In the past decade, films like *Padmaavat* faced attacks from certain groups. There has been a rising trend of boycotting films featuring Muslim protagonists, while appeals to watch films with Hindu protagonists have increased. However, the impact of boycott culture can be paradoxical. Hits like *Pathaan* and war films find success, while films like *Adipurush* may face failure.' He goes on to point out that, 'The results reflect public sentiment. At times, capitalist forces seem to triumph, while at other times, they face setbacks. The ebb and flow of success and failure in the boycott culture hint at the complex dynamics of societal preferences. This phenomenon isn't just about avoiding or supporting certain films; it becomes a societal survey, reflecting the multifaceted nature of public opinions. In this nuanced landscape, the power dynamics between capitalist interests and public sentiment play out, shaping the fate of films. The boycott culture, therefore, is not a one-dimensional force; it's a complex interplay of politics, society, and cinematic choices that ultimately reflect the diverse perspectives within the community.'

Curiously, a recent investigation by the *Washington Post* revealed that the OTT industry is also allegedly facing pressure when green-lighting projects with political or religious themes. Film-maker Anurag Kashyap spoke of 'invisible censorship' on streaming platforms when Netflix decided not to move forward with his adaptation of the non-fiction book *Maximum City*, which explores the themes of 'Hindu bigotry and the extremes of hope and despair in Mumbai'.[6]

Film critic and author Mayank Shekhar makes some important observations on this OTT trend while pointing out that politics and religion are no-go areas on OTT. Delving into the history of how OTT censorship took shape, he points out that one of the reasons for this was the disproportionate response from the state to the Amazon Prime Video series *Tandav*. 'There was literally nothing in that series worth offence. But a precedent was set, where the UP Police came down to Mumbai to arrest Prime Video executives, basis an FIR on an individual's complaint—because somebody's religious sentiment had been hurt.' He goes on to add that 'shortly thereafter the government imposed a new set of IT rules, with no precedence in a mature/ real democracy, placing internet censorship under its direct ambit, specifically OTT content, social media and online news.'

The new rules were framed for online intermediaries in February 2021, augmenting existing government control over online platforms. As per these rules, social media companies need to take down content within thirty-six hours of receiving a government notice. They also need to appoint a nodal person for 24×7 coordination with law-enforcement officials. The rules, however, go far beyond just social media. The central government can ask 'curated content platforms' such as Netflix to take down or modify content. The same applies to digital news platforms.

Speaking of the action taken post the complaint against *Tandav*, Shekhar adds, 'You watch such a frightening farce play out, with the state/government as the primary actor, everyone exercises overt caution.' Speaking of overt caution, it is worth mentioning that film critic Namrata Joshi had posted on social media the details of an instruction manual she had received that came with a link to the preview of a show called *Grahan*. The review instructions mentioned that the show should not be connected to any current or past political happening, while the reviewer was free to comment on aspects of the show such as its dialogue and cinematography, etc. This, from a platform that had green-lighted the show based on the Sikh riots of 1984!

Shekhar points out that there has been a slew of political content that has been aborted in the past, out of the fear of the government, ruling party and its affiliates coming down heavily on a platform if they don't agree with a fact on screen, or a point of view in general. He points out several instances—Shah Rukh Khan was scripting a series, presumably along the lines of *House of Cards*, to do with Lutyens' Delhi; Anurag Kashyap had been sanctioned the screen adaptation of Suketu Mehta's *Maximum City* (focusing on the 1992 Bombay riots); Irrfan Khan starred in a series by Gursimran Khamba called *Gormint*; Dibakar Banerjee had a political film ready for Netflix—all of which were aborted. Furthermore, he points out how law firms have film departments in place that vet scripts to pluck out any reference to anything, anywhere, that could potentially cause a problem to an OTT platform. 'Such is the level of self-censorship on a nascent medium like streaming that really kicked off in India with a lot of promise,' he says. 'Now, with excessive fear of individuals and groups taking offence, the state potentially striking its whip, other commercial constraints, to simply issues of talent, R&D, technology, budgets—it's a miracle that anything good gets made at all,' opines Shekhar.

The other effect that the boycott/cancel culture has had, according to Shekhar, is on the stars and celebrities, particularly with reference to their opening up on anything at all. Even on their own lives. 'There is this constant pressure of playing safe, lest there be a statement that is spun out of context to destroy their reputation or casually shame them in public. The publicists have been rendered equally paranoid. The Sushant Singh Rajput death, and the level of scavenging done by the mainstream television media and social media handles partially reversed the relationship between film stars/celebrities and the public at large, and the news media in particular,' he says.

While former Union Information and Broadcasting Minister Anurag Thakur deplored the 'boycott culture', making a public statement saying that it vitiates the atmosphere at a time when India is keen to enhance its influence as a soft power. Artists and film-makers alike continue to feel the brunt.

Is there a way, then, to end these calls for boycott? The straightforward answer seems to be 'no, we can't'. It's a free society, after all. What then is the way forward? For Sudhir Mishra, it is the fact that 'You have to say some stuff without being afraid. You may have to change the way you say something. You might have to twist your words to get your idea across. But if you give up, then that would be the end of it.'

Amidst all this, a ray of hope is ignited by film-maker Vipul Amrutlal Shah, who feels that the boycott trend is temporary. 'The boycott culture was a reaction to certain things that people were unhappy with in our popular culture. I do not think that it can be a permanent trend. Boycott culture to my mind has come to its natural end. There can be a sporadic incident of one film or one book or one something, but that's where it will end. It won't last beyond that.' Now that is something we need to wait and watch.

Chapter 11

The Legend of Ram

Time: Sometime in January 2024

Place: Family WhatsApp group

Somnath: So happy to be witnessing these times. Just wanted to share my happiness with you, my family.

Raghav: I so agree, bhaisahab. The entire nation's mood is pulsating and exuberant.

Sudesh: Yes, it already feels like Deepawali all over again. I can't wait to see what 22 January will look like.

Somnath: Yes. Crores of families are celebrating the return of Shri Ram to his rightful abode.

Raghav: I am also happy to see that the myth of Shri Ram being a 'north Indian' phenomenon has been shattered. Prime

---

This WhatsApp group is demonstrative of the popular outpourings and messages that were in circulation during these events. The participants in the chat are fictional. Any similarity to actual persons, living or dead, is purely coincidental.

Minister Modi's recent pilgrimage to various temples in south India has shown how Shri Ram is the common binding factor for India.

Reyansh: Uncle, but don't you think the ceremony has been turned into a political spectacle by the BJP to earn electoral brownie points?

Somnath: I don't think so at all. The Opposition is making this huge fuss when they were the ones who first denied the existence of Lord Ram and now are claiming they are worried about the spiritual essence of the mandir being eroded by politics. I think it is important for you young minds not to be corrupted by such influences.

Raghav: Absolutely. We do not need to wear the pretentious mask of separating Church and State like the West. Let us all keep our attention focused on the grandest event of our times—the pran pratishtha ceremony, and not be sidetracked.

* * *

Day Zero—22 January 2024

According to Hindu mythology, Lord Ram was born in Ayodhya at the confluence of *Abhijit Muhurat, Mrigashirsha Nakshatra, Amrit Siddhi Yoga* and *Sarvartha Siddhi Yoga*. All these auspicious periods seemed to align on 22 January 2024, making it the ideal date for the pran pratishtha or the consecration ceremony of the Ram Mandir at Ayodhya. The idol of Ram Lalla or infant Lord Ram, sculpted by renowned sculptor Arun Yogiraj from *shyamal* (dark) stone that was 2.5 billion years old, was to find a home at the new Ram Temple.

According to one count, there are as many as 6,48,000 temples in India. Yet a temple to mark the birthplace of Lord Ram in Ayodhya held a special place in the hearts of millions of devotees. It was here that the epic tale of Lord Ram had unfolded, adding spiritual significance to the city; besides, the site of the Ram Temple had also been the site of a fractious issue that went back more than a century. It was no surprise then that in the days preceding the consecration ceremony, the city of Ayodhya received a complete makeover as it got ready to celebrate the 'return' of Lord Ram. In the run-up to the D-Day, while special spiritual ceremonies were organized in Ayodhya, the entire country had an air of festivity, soaked as it was with Ram bhajans—devotional songs in praise of the Lord. Prime Minister Narendra Modi himself had posted about half a dozen such devotional songs on social media, each of them singing paeans to Lord Ram making a homecoming—*Ram aayenge.*

On the appointed day, the central government announced half-day closing at all central government offices, central institutions and central industrial establishments 'to enable employees to participate in the celebrations'. Some 10,000 people attended the ceremony at Ayodhya, including movie stars, politicians, athletes, spiritual leaders, businesspeople, media personnel besides foreign dignitaries. NRIs from fifty-five countries including Argentina, Australia, Canada, France, Germany, Japan, the USA and many others attended the event. Notable among the invitees were a US-based oncologist, a senior fellow at the Nokia Bell Labs in Indiana, a Norwegian MP, a New Zealand scientist, a Fijian industrialist and saints who have established Hindu schools in the Caribbean. People across religions, geographies and social identities joined in to celebrate the historic event. Lakhs of others watched the live telecast of the ceremony in their homes as also in temples across the country. Noted film actor Anupam Kher, in speaking to us, pointed out how on the flight to Ayodhya he had witnessed an experience like never before with chants of '*Ram naam*' filling the skies. 'Sometimes a religious place can become a great place of togetherness, harmony and progression. Ayodhya deserves to become the most popular religious destination just as Vatican City is. *Ayodhya se ek naye adhyay ki shuruat hogi* (Ayodhya will herald the beginning of a new chapter),' he went on to add. All over the city, the sentiments were similar. Abhinav, a nine-year-old, who performs *Ram Katha*, spoke for millions of others when he called the event 'the end of Shri Ram's 500 years of *vanvaas*' while also reminding us that the meaning of Ayodhya is invincible—'*jisse yudh mein jeeta na ja sake*'.

There was a remarkable energy in Ayodhya. The atmosphere echoed with the sounds of conch shells and mantras creating a spiritually charged ambience. It was like Diwali being celebrated all over again. There was palpable excitement in the air as army helicopters showered flower petals on the newly constructed Ram Temple.

Author Amish Tripathi confessed that he had tears in his eyes on seeing the idol of Ram Lalla. 'It is a powerful, *jagrut murti*,' he said, visibly in awe. Arun Yogiraj, the sculptor, Tripathi feels, has the blessings of the Lord to be able to create an idol that makes you feel protected and awestruck at the same time. It is interesting to note how Arun Yogiraj in speaking to us had said he had gone through thousands of pictures of Lord Ram in trying to bring together the divinity and innocence of a five-year-old in the idol. Vijetha, his wife, had earlier told us that while sculpting the idol, Yogiraj had prayed to the god to reveal his face through his work.

Tripathi goes on to speak of how Ayodhya will change India and the world. 'Lord Ram is a symbol of sacrifice, grace and self-control. Heroes and gods that we look up to say something about the culture of the land as well. Here was a king who put his land and people above everything including his family. The message is for us to build an India that Lord Ram would be proud of,' he opines. He further goes on to add that this historic moment can mean a lot for civilization and time. Speaking of Indian culture in particular, he mentions how 'India's way of thinking isn't in binaries'. He feels that India is among the few cultures that believes in mutual respect. And that this is a message that India needs to give out to the world.

PM Modi prostrating before the idol during the ceremony is among the many images that took the internet by storm. 'Our Ram has come,' Modi said in his address following the consecration. He went on to add that he could still feel the divine vibrations he had experienced during the consecration ceremony inside the sanctum sanctorum of the Ram Temple. 'This temple is not just a mere shrine; it is the manifestation of Bharat's vision, philosophy and insight,' he said. 'It is a temple of national consciousness in the form of Lord Ram. Ram is the faith of Bharat; Ram is the foundation of Bharat. Ram is the thought of Bharat; Ram is the constitution of Bharat. Ram is the consciousness of Bharat,' he went on to say.[1]

Congratulatory messages poured in from all over the world in the wake of the inauguration, including from world leaders. Taiwan's minister of foreign affairs, Joseph Wu, said that the world is divided into two types of people: 'Those who are going to fall in love with India and those who already have.'[2] New Zealand's minister for regulation, David Seymour, complimented PM Modi when he said that '. . . it was his leadership that made this construction possible after 500 years.

The temple is majestic and built to last another 1000 years.'[3]
Besides visuals of the Ram Temple, many people also shared
visuals of the Indian diaspora celebrating the pran pratishtha
ceremony in foreign lands—be it lighting up Times Square in
New York with Lord Ram's illustration or devotees chanting Jai
Shri Ram at the iconic Eiffel Tower.

Temple of Development

Other than the religious impact, the city of Ayodhya has fast
become a temple of development. Besides the construction of
the grand Ram Temple, a work of art that displays remarkable
architectural finesse in the traditional Nagara style, the entire
city of Ayodhya has received a massive infrastructure push.
Whether it is the clean ghats along the River Sarayu or the
wide roads, residents view the city as a representation of heaven
on earth. Annu Bhai Sompura, in charge of Shri Ram Mandir
Karyashala, spoke of how Ayodhya had undergone a huge
transformation from the time when the city received electricity
for only four hours a day. 'Kitni sarkarein aayi gayi, kisi ne kuch
nahi kiya. Jab Modi aaye hume pata tha mandir banega. Woh
lohpurush hai, kisi se darta nahi (Many governments changed
but no one did anything. When Modi was elected we knew
the temple would be built. He is an ironman who isn't scared
of anyone).' His views were echoed by many residents of the
city. Amit Manjhi, a boatman who has spent twelve years in
his profession, looked at the construction of the temple as a
huge boost to tourism. Equipped to accept digital payments,
he stands testimony to the development the city has seen.
Om Prakash Pandey, a priest at Sarayu Ghat who has been
living there for thirty-five-odd years, in speaking to us of the
development, said that Ayodhya had turned into heaven—
'Swarg ban gaya hai Ayodhya'. He goes on to reminisce about

how earning 10 or 20 rupees a day was once difficult but how now earning 400 to 500 rupees a day has been made possible. Acharya Satyendra Das, the chief priest of the temple in 1992, in speaking of the infrastructure push, went a step further to state how Ram rajya was about to return. *'Ab woh anand aayega jo Ram rajya mein tha* (we will witness the same joy as was there during Lord Ram's reign).'

Their enthusiasm wasn't misplaced. While religion and development are traditionally seen as being mutually exclusive, the making of the Ram Mandir at Ayodhya has given a huge fillip to business and the city's economy.

Data by the Uttar Pradesh Tourism Department shows that while 3,25,000 tourists visited Ayodhya in 2021, the number surged to 23.9 million the following year.[4] With the ancient city transforming into a global religious hotspot, it holds the power of revolutionizing the economy of not just Ayodhya but also of more than a dozen neighbouring districts. In fact, with increased tourist spending in the state, the Uttar Pradesh government is set to earn an additional Rs 20,000 crore to Rs 25,000 crore in tax revenue in FY25, as per an SBI research report.[5]

Besides the temple complex, Ayodhya has attracted funding for a host of development and infrastructure projects, which will not only boost tourism in and around the city but also turn the city into a regional growth hub. The $175 million Ayodhya airport was built in less than two years and can handle around 10 lakh passengers, to start with. In addition, the newly redeveloped Ayodhya Dham railway station, other rail projects and civic infrastructure projects were also announced. Addressing a public meeting in Ayodhya, Prime Minister Narendra Modi had earlier stated, 'the foundation stone of development works worth more than Rs 15000 crore has been laid and inaugurated here.[6] These infrastructure-related works will once again establish modern Ayodhya with pride on the map of the country. Today's India is beautifying its pilgrimage sites and is also immersed in the world of digital technology.'

As per the master plan of 2031, the redevelopment of Ayodhya is expected to be completed over ten years with an investment of over Rs 85,000 crore.[7] The design vision is reported to include modern facilities and amenities while celebrating the history and culture of the ancient city. In fact, development and infrastructure projects in the city have been categorized into eight broad themes—Aesthetic Ayodhya, Clean Ayodhya, Efficient Ayodhya, Accessible Ayodhya, Experiential Ayodhya, Modern Ayodhya, Cultural Ayodhya and Healthy Ayodhya.

It is a testament to the estimated potential of the city that everyone, from real estate developers to airlines to the country's leading corporate houses, is heading to the temple town, which wasn't on their radar till a few years ago. Ayodhya's rising tourism has also beckoned luxury hotel giants. Indian Hotels Company Ltd (IHCL), for instance, has signed management contracts for two new properties in Ayodhya—a 100-room Vivanta hotel and a 120-room Ginger hotel. ITC Ltd—a leading player in the luxury- and mid-segment hotels business—is also in discussions with developers to offer branding and management solutions for their assets under development. OYO, the country's largest hotel chain operator, plans to add fifty hotels and homes, aggregating to some 1000 rooms in Ayodhya, as per media reports.

Fast-moving consumer goods (FMCG) companies and food service chains had already made a beeline for Ayodhya ahead of the Ram Temple consecration on 22 January.

To tap into the sudden increase in demand, major brands in the consumer space have also upped the ante to ensure visibility for their products.

Not only do all domestic roads seem to be leading to Ayodhya right now, but the government also plans to put the 'Land of Shree Ram' on the world tourism map.

Bimlendra Mohan Pratap Mishra, a descendant of the raja of Ayodhya, sums up the prevailing sentiment in Ayodhya when he says that legend has it that Ma Sita had given a *shrap* (curse) to Ayodhya when she was sent to the jungle by Lord Rama. '*Ab lagta hai Ma Sita prasann hai aur shrap wapas le liya hai. Vaibhav wapas aa raha hai.*' Prosperity is returning, he says with a sense of finality.

* * *

'Ayodhya Ram Mandir Case Judgement: Supreme Court Rules in Favour of Ram Lalla'

November 2019

22 January 2024 was presaged when on 9 November 2019 a five-judge Supreme Court bench led by then chief justice Ranjan Gogoi read out a landmark judgment ruling in favour of the Ram Temple being constructed, giving the ownership of the disputed 2.77-acre tract of land in Ayodhya to the Ram Janmabhoomi Trust. It also ruled that an alternative 5-acre plot will be found for a mosque in the holy town in Uttar Pradesh.

The Ram Janmabhoomi dispute had been a contentious matter for many years, entangled in numerous court actions by Muslim and Hindu religious groups. The Supreme Court's judgment did, in fact, overturn the judgment of the Allahabad High Court, which had divided the Ram Janmabhoomi–Babri Masjid site into three parts, with the Sunni Waqf Board, Nirmohi Akhara and Ram Lalla each receiving a third of it. The Supreme Court, while delivering its verdict in 2019, stated the Allahabad High Court had 'completely erred' in its ruling.

In the preceding years, the Ram Temple issue had become a multifaceted confluence of public sentiment, historical significance and political manoeuvring. For decades, the issue had been a focal point of tension and controversy, leading to both communal riots and political strife.

While the Ayodhya Ram Janmabhoomi dispute traces its origins to as far back as 1852, the beginnings of the temple movement, in fact, can be traced back to certain archaeological studies that were conducted in more recent times. An excavation headed by archaeologist B.B. Lal in 1975–76, for instance, claimed to have found the remains of a columned Hindu temple beneath the existing structure. K.K. Muhammad, the only Muslim who participated in the study, in speaking to us, pointed out that he had seen 'pillars on which *purna kalasha*, the Hindu symbol of prosperity, were present'. He goes on to add how it became his 'moral duty to speak the truth' when in 1990, historians led by those at JNU, Delhi and Aligarh Muslim universities came out with a false report that insinuated that there was no need to hand over the site to the Hindus. This, he says, despite the fact that it was a politically incorrect decision personally for him as he was a government servant and still on his probation period, and therefore could be dismissed without as much as a show cause notice. When threatened with suspension, he says he responded that he was doing his duty and that even if the consequence of performing his duty was death, he would welcome it.[8]

Given these developments, the BJP went on to organize what was by far the biggest movement around building the Ram Temple in the nineties. It is impossible to imagine the Ram Janmabhoomi movement without senior BJP leader L.K. Advani, whose 'rath yatra' changed the course of Indian politics. On 25 September 1990, Advani embarked on this yatra from Somnath in Gujarat to Ayodhya in UP to make people aware of the Ram Janmabhoomi issue and to raise support for the call to build a Ram Temple in Ayodhya. The yatra, which was seen as the biggest mass mobilization of Hindutva forces, went on to whip up a strong Hindu fervour, besides increasing the party's vote bank. In fact, the yatra, or what came to be known as the kamandal politics of Hindutva, became the perfect foil for the Opposition's Mandal agitation. The yatra ultimately paved the way for the demolition of the Babri Masjid on 6 December 1992, when thousands of 'kar sevaks', who claimed that an ancient Ram Temple had once stood at the disputed site, brought down the sixteenth-century Babri Masjid in Ayodhya, leading to one of the most gruesome incidences of sectarian violence in India's history.

It was PM Modi's ascent to power in 2014 that marked a significant shift in Indian politics. The promise to build the Ram Temple in Ayodhya was a central plank of the BJP's election manifesto, tapping into deep-seated religious sentiments among a significant section of the Indian population. Modi's role in advancing the cause of the Ram Temple was instrumental in solidifying his support base among Hindu nationalists, who viewed him as a decisive leader willing to take bold steps to assert India's Hindu identity. The Supreme Court's ruling, which granted the land to Hindu groups for the construction of the temple while providing an alternative site for the Muslim community to build a mosque, was hailed as a victory by Hindu nationalists and a validation of their long-standing demand. Modi's government swiftly moved to set up a trust for the construction of the temple, signalling its commitment to fulfilling its electoral promise.

The groundbreaking ceremony for the commencement of the construction of the Ram Mandir, held in August 2020 amidst much fanfare, was a momentous occasion that further bolstered Modi's image as a leader who delivered on his promises. The event, attended by top BJP leaders and Hindu religious figures, was broadcast live across the country, evoking a sense of pride and triumph among millions. Modi's participation in the ceremony, where he laid the foundation stone for the temple, was seen as a symbolic endorsement of the Hindu nationalist agenda.

Religious Symbolism or Political Calculation?

Critics, however, saw it as a testament to Modi's political astuteness in harnessing religious symbolism for electoral gains. Many saw the Ram Temple inauguration as marking an unofficial start to his re-election campaign as the event, poised on the precipice of a looming general election, seemed to transcend the boundaries of religion alone. To many, therefore, the Ram Temple inauguration was a calculated move in the delicate dance of politics.

The temple, which sits at the heart of the Hindu narrative, also fuelled debates around issues of secularism, minority rights and the role of religion in public life. While supporters celebrated it as a historic moment of cultural revival and national unity, critics raised concerns about the marginalization of religious minorities and the erosion of India's secular fabric, while pointing out that historically, India's democracy has thrived on the inclusion of diverse voices. They felt that the Ram Temple event represented an unprecedented assertion by the state of the majority religion's cultural and historical pre-eminence.

Critics also pointed out that the construction of the Ram Temple had overshadowed pressing issues such as economic development, social justice and governance, raising questions about the government's priorities and its commitment to inclusive nation-building.

As for the political ramifications of the temple's construction—they were multifaceted. On the one hand, it solidified the BJP's position as the vanguard of Hindu nationalism, further bolstering its support base. On the other, it presented a challenge to opposition parties, forcing them to navigate a delicate balance between respecting religious sentiments and upholding constitutional principles. In fact, the opposition alliance did not appear to have any concrete plan to counter the strong narrative around the Ram Temple, with most of India's opposition parties declining the invite to the event, saying it did not befit a secular India. The biggest challenge that presented itself before the Opposition was therefore to establish its own narrative without being seen as anti-Hindu.

What is interesting to note here is also that the Narendra Modi-led BJP did not restrict the fervour to a single temple. In fact, in the run-up to the consecration ceremony, Prime Minister Narendra Modi embarked on a Ramayana trail—a yatra of the temples linked with Lord Rama, as told in the Ramayana. 'It is said that to participate in a ceremony like the consecration, one must try to feel a part of the divine force within oneself,'[9] Prime Minister Narendra Modi said as he undertook a special eleven-day ritual ahead of the pran pratishtha ceremony on 22 January. He travelled from Maharashtra to Andhra Pradesh to Kerala to Tamil Nadu, with his temple visits in these destinations interestingly corresponding with the sequence of events in the Ramayana. He began with the Kalaram Temple in Panchavati in Maharashtra's Nashik. While the name Panchavati means the land of five banyan trees, the Kalaram Temple derives its name from the fact that Lord Ram used his *kala roop* to slay 14,000 demons. Panchvati was the place where Lord Ram first settled during his exile and from where Sita was abducted. PM Modi offered his prayers there and listened to the *Bhavartha Ramayana* written in Marathi. He then travelled over 1000 kilometres to

Lepakshi in Andhra Pradesh where he visited the Veerbhadra Temple, the place where Jatayu was wounded while trying to rescue Sita from Ravan. There he listened to the *Ranganatha Ramayana*, the Telegu rendition of the Ramayana. His next visit was to Kerala's Thrissur district, where he visited the Sri Ramaswami Temple. Legend has it that after meeting Jatayu, Lord Ram reached the kingdom of the *vanara*s, Kishkindha, where he met Hanuman and Sugriva, the king of Kishkindha. Later on, Hanuman found Sita imprisoned in Ashok Vatika and delivered Lord Rama's message to her and offered to rescue her. Sita refused as she was waiting for Lord Ram alone to come and save her as well as avenge her insult at the hands of Ravan. Hanuman came back bearing a ring that Sita had asked him to give Lord Ram. PM Modi's next stop was at Srirangam in Tamil Nadu's Trichy. It is believed that Lord Ram gifted an idol of Vishnu to Vibhishana, the younger brother of Ravana, as a sign of gratitude for helping him during the Lanka war against his brother, with the instruction to never keep the idol on the ground or it would become permanently fixed there. When Vibhishana was travelling through Tiruchirappalli, he stopped to have a bath and entrusted the idol to a local boy who was actually Ganesha. When he returned, he saw the idol on the ground. Thousands of years later, a king of the Chola dynasty found the idol there and built the Ranganathaswamy Temple. From Trichy, the PM went on to Rameswaram, where he visited the famous Arulmigu Ramanathaswamy Temple—one of the Char Dhams, a set of four Hindu pilgrimage sites in India.

It is believed that when Lord Ram was returning to India from Lanka after having defeated and killed Ravana, he wanted to atone for the sin of killing a Brahmin (Ravana). He was advised by Lord Shiva to make a *shivling* and perform a puja. Lord Ram then sent Hanuman to Mount Kailasa, the abode of Lord Shiva, to find a shivling. However, Hanuman was delayed on his return, and ultimately Sita used sand from the seashore to craft a shivling. The PM finally visited Dhanushkodi, where he performed a puja at the Kothandaramaswamy Temple. It is believed that Lord Ram used his bow and arrow to destroy the Ram Sethu, the bridge constructed by Lord Rama and his vanara army to cross over to Lanka to rescue Sita, while on his way back to Ayodhya. It is also believed to be the place where Lord Ram conducted Vibhishan's coronation.

While critics saw this Ramayana yatra as Modi's subtle outreach to south India ahead of the 2024 elections, the exercise was projected as his effort to unify the country under a common cultural identity. In fact, the heritage issue has been underlined on several occasions by PM Modi. In his second term, he repeatedly spoke about doing away with the signs of colonialism and slavery and re-establishing Indian tradition and heritage. Apart from redeveloping significant religious sites including the Mahakal corridor, Kedarnath and Varanasi, he claimed to give a proper place to Hindu traditions by way of various initiatives. The establishment of the new Parliament building was also seen as a part of this initiative. In this sequence, the biggest act was the consecration of the Ram Temple. In fact, a senior BJP leader was quoted as saying that while the Viksit Bharat Sankalp Yatra had been launched to make India a developed nation by 2047, the pran pratishtha ceremony of the Ram Temple provided the opportunity to once again take pride in India's glorious history.

To Sum Up

While the inauguration of the Ram Temple could have been the crowning glory for BJP's brand of politics, things turned out differently. The event on 22 January garnered attention for its scale, projecting the BJP to potentially surpass 400 seats in the upcoming General Elections. In fact, this narrative was even embraced prematurely by opposition leaders. However, both democracy and sports share the uncertainty that one shouldn't jump to conclusions until the final outcome is determined—it's a risky proposition to assume final truths prematurely, and this case was no exception.

The monumental event in Ayodhya that day was hailed as a pivotal moment for the BJP, crafting a narrative of triumph that resonated nationwide. Yet beneath this celebration simmered a subdued discontent. Rakesh Parmar, a small kirana shop owner in Ayodhya, observed that while everyone else seemed to partake in the festivities, the local residents were left out. Reflecting on the event, he questioned how the development touted would benefit them if they had no homes or employment left.

Sushila Devi, a long-time resident of Ayodhya, expressed a sentiment of simplicity and compassion associated with Lord Ram. She emphasized Ram's role in empathizing with people's sorrows and embodying virtue, underscoring the lack of connection felt by locals as they saw themselves sidelined in the grand narratives spun in Ram's name. This sentiment of exclusion became palpable by 4 June.

The discontent among Ayodhya residents highlights a broader issue: while political spectacles may create impressive narratives, they often fail to address the practical concerns of the people directly affected. Development must be inclusive, addressing the needs of all stakeholders, to truly resonate positively. As Ayodhya's story unfolds, it serves as a poignant reminder of the importance of balancing political symbolism with tangible benefits for local communities, ensuring that progress is meaningful and equitable for all.

Notes

Prologue

1 Chandrajit Mitra, 'Exit Polls Drive Markets to Record High, Investors Richer by ₹ 12 Lakh Crore', NDTV, 3 June 2024, https://www.ndtv.com/india-news/massive-jump-in-stock-market-after-exit-polls-predict-big-bjp-win-5804282, accessed on 22 July 2024.

2 https://www.ndtv.com/india-news/lok-sabha-elections-2024-sympathy-wave-for-uddhav-thackeray-sharad-pawar-chhagan-bhujbal-5538107

3 India Today, 'Priyanka Gandhi Jabs PM: "Why Ask for Votes on Basis of Mangalsutra, Religion?"', *India Today*, 18 May 2024, https://www.indiatoday.in/elections/lok-sabha/story/priyanka-gandhi-interview-pm-modi-mangalsutra-religion-votes-unemployment-2540808-2024-05-18, 23 July 2024.

4 Derek O'Brien, 'How Digital Platforms Overtook Traditional Media to Reach the Voters this Election', *Indian Express*, 7 June 2024, https://indianexpress.com/article/opinion/columns/how-digital-platforms-overtook-traditional-media-to-reach-the-voters-this-election-9376854/, accessed on 23 July 2024.

5 Ambika Pandit, 'Big Message Is People Don't Want Modi, Shah Running Country: Rahul Gandhi', *Times of India*, 4 June 2024, https://timesofindia.indiatimes.com/india/

big-message-is-people-dont-want-modi-shah-running-country-rahul-gandhi/articleshow/110714057.cms, accessed on 23 July 2024.

6   https://www.livemint.com/elections/exit-polls-2024-bjp-may-beat-tmc-in-west-bengal-pollsters-predict-16-lok-sabha-seats-for-mamata-banerjees-party-11717252758140.html

Chapter 1: JNU: Split Down the Middle

1   Express News Service, 'JNU Row-Feb 9 and After: Authorities Present Their Side of Story, *Indian Express*, 18 February 2019, https://indianexpress.com/article/india/india-news-india/jnu-row-feb-9-and-after-authorities-present-their-side-of-story/, accessed on 19 July 2024.

2   Yuthika Bhargava, 'JNU Branded "Anti-national" by Google Maps', *The Hindu*, 25 March 2016, https://www.thehindu.com/news/national/googlemaps-search-for-antinational-patriotism-leads-to-jnu/article8396695.ece, accessed on 19 July 2024.

3   Agencies and TNN, 'Rahul Gandhi Visits JNU, Says Those Suppressing Institution's Voice Are Anti-national', *Times of India*, 13 February 2016, https://timesofindia.indiatimes.com/india/rahul-gandhi-visits-jnu-says-those-suppressing-institutions-voice-are-anti-national/articleshow/50976332.cms, accessed on 19 July 2024.

4   Agencies, '"Traitor, Anti-national and Intolerant": Who Said What at JNU Protest', *Hindustan Times*, 16 February 2016, https://www.hindustantimes.com/india/traitor-anti-national-and-intolerant-who-said-what-at-the-jnu-protest/story-zFhiONmAl93OETobVEjAHK.html, accessed on 19 July 2024.

5   PTI, 'Amit Shah Accuses Rahul Gandhi of Supporting "Anti-Nationals"', *Indian Express*, 15 February 2016,

https://indianexpress.com/article/india/india-news-india/amit-shahs-rahul-gandhi-jnu-blog-heres-what-he-has-to-say-about-jnu-incident-and-congress-party/, accessed on 19 July 2024.

6   Rakesh Mohan Chaturvedi, 'Jan Swabhiman Abhiyan: Inspired by JNU Stir, BJP to Take Nationalism Debate to Masses', *Economic Times*, 17 February 2016, https://economictimes.indiatimes.com/news/politics-and-nation/jan-swabhiman-abhiyan-inspired-by-jnu-stir-bjp-to-take-nationalism-debate-to-masses/articleshow/51016558.cms?from=mdr, accessed on 19 July 2024.

7   PTI, 'JNU Home to "Anti-national" Forces, Claims RSS Mouthpiece', *Times of India*, 3 November 2015, https://timesofindia.indiatimes.com/india/jnu-home-to-anti-national-forces-claims-rss-mouthpiece/articleshow/49639653.cms, accessed on 19 July 2024.

8   India Today Web Desk, 'Have No Information on Tukde Tukde Gang: Home Ministry in RTI Reply', *India Today*, 20 January 2020, https://www.indiatoday.in/india/story/have-no-information-on-tukde-tukde-gang-home-ministry-in-rti-reply-1638593-2020-01-20, accessed on 19 July 2024.

9   Vasudha Mukherjee, 'The Mandal Commission Decoded: How OBC Reservation Came into Effect', *Business Standard*, 20 October 2023, https://www.business-standard.com/india-news/the-mandal-commission-decoded-how-obc-reservation-came-into-effect-123102000445_1.html, accessed on 19 July 2024.

10 Santosh Desai, 'Of Politics and Culture', *Times of India* blog, 20 December 2020, https://timesofindia.indiatimes.com/blogs/Citycitybangbang/of-politics-and-culture/, accessed on 19 July 2024.

Chapter 2: Large-Scale Protests: A New Playbook

1   Sanjeeb Mukherjee, '75% Farmers Want to Quit, Says CSDS, Lokniti Survey', *Business Standard*, 11 March 2014, https://www.business-standard.com/article/elections-2014/75-farmers-want-to-quit-says-csds-lokniti-survey-1140311 00896_1.html, accessed on 19 July 2024.

2   The Hindu Bureau, 'Growth Dips, Public Investment Stagnant in Agriculture Sector', *The Hindu*, 1 February 2023, https://www.thehindu.com/business/agri-business/economic-survey-2022-23-growth-dips-public-investment-stagnant-in-agriculture-sector/article66455088.ece#:~:text=The%20Economic%20Survey%20noted%20that,5.5%25%20in%202019%2D20, accessed on 19 July 2024.

3   https://x.com/rihanna/status/1356625889602199552?lang=en

4   Akhilesh Sharma, 'Unprecedented Reaction by Government to Tweets by Rihanna, Other Celebs', NDTV, 3 February 2021, https://www.ndtv.com/india-news/farmers-protest-government-says-temptation-of-sensationalist-comments-especially-by-celebrities-others-not-accurate-2362280, accessed on 19 July 2024.

5   IANS, 'Decision Only Because of Upcoming Polls, Says Priyanka Gandhi Vadra', *Business-Standard*, 19 November 2021, https://www.business-standard.com/article/current-affairs/decision-only-because-of-upcoming-polls-says-priyanka-gandhi-vadra-121111900524_1.html, accessed on 19 July 2024.

6   Jelvin Jose, 'The Farmers' Movement and "Anti-National" Messaging in India', South Asian Voices, 18 March 2021,

https://southasianvoices.org/the-farmers-movement-and-anti-national-messaging-in-india/, accessed on 19 July 2024.

7 Anon, 'Swaminathan Report: National Commission on Farmers', PRS Legislative Research, n.d., https://prsindia.org/policy/report-summaries/swaminathan-report-national-commission-farmers, accessed on 19 July 2024.

8 BBC News, 'Vinesh Phogat: Protesting India Wrestlers Say Police Assaulted Them', BBC, 4 May 2023, https://www.bbc.com/news/world-asia-india-65478542#:~:text=%22The%20way%20they%20have%20made,official%20was%20drunk%20on%20site, accessed on 19 July 2024.

9 Sabi Hussain, 'Sports Ministry Suspends Newly-elected WFI, Asks IOA to Form Panel, Brij Bhushan Says "done" with Wrestling', *Times of India*, 15 December 2023, https://timesofindia.indiatimes.com/sports/more-sports/wrestling/government-suspends-wfi-over-blatant-violation-of-procedural-norms/articleshow/106254324.cms, accessed on 19 July 2024.

Chapter 3: Balakot Air Strikes; New Wave of Nationalism

1 Sunil Prabhu, 'India Strikes after Pulwama Terror Attack, Hits Biggest Jaish-e-Mohammed Camp in Balakot', NDTV, 26 February 2019, https://www.ndtv.com/india-news/india-struck-biggest-training-camp-of-jaish-in-balakot-large-number-of-terrorists-eliminated-governm-1999390, accessed on 19 July 2024.

2 Special Correspondent, 'India Struck Biggest Training Camp of JeM—Full Statement from Foreign Secretary Vijay Gokhale', *The Hindu*, 9 June 2020, https://www.thehindu.com/news/national/india-struck-biggest-training-camp-of-

jem-foreign-sec-confirms/article26372319.ece, accessed on 19 July 2024.

3   ABP NEWS, 'PM Modi's Chest Measures 156 Inches: Ram Vilas Paswan | ABP News', 3 March 2019, YouTube, https://www.youtube.com/watch?v=6S6Cc89H73M, accessed on 19 July 2024.

4   Asian News International, '"Did We Really Attack": Congress Leader Sam Pitroda Questions Balakot Strike', *Hindustan Times*, 24 April 2020, https://www. hindustantimes.com/india-news/did-we-really-attack-congress-leader-sam-pitroda-questions-balakot-strike/ story-XxzNIXZe2TQiZXEyKWR0uO.html, accessed on 19 July 2024.

5   ABPL, 'Modi Slams Opposition for Doubting Balakot Air Strike', ABPL, n.d., https://www.asian-voice.com/News/ India/Modi-slams-opposition-for-doubting-Balakot-air-strike, accessed on 19 July 2024.

6   India Today Web Desk, 'Pulwama, Balakot Examples of How BJP Used National Security to Profit: Shashi Tharoor', *India Today*, 21 September 2019, https://www.indiatoday.in/india/ story/pulwama-balakot-bjp-national-security-profit-shashi-tharoor-1601489-2019-09-20, accessed on 19 July 2024.

7   Pranav Gupta and Dishil Shrimankar, 'How Nationalism Helped the BJP', india-seminar.com, n.d., https://www. india-seminar.com/2019/720/720_pranav_and_dishil. htm, accessed on 19 July 2024.

8   Pavan K. Varma, 'Nationalism Vs Patriotism: Nationalism's Cynical Misuse, Conflating Dissent with Sedition, Devalues Our Ever', *Times of India* Blog, 29 March 2019, https://timesofindia.indiatimes.com/blogs/toi-edit-page/ nationalism-vs-patriotism-nationalisms-cynical-misuse-conflating-dissent-with-sedition-devalues-our-everyday-patriotism/, accessed on 22 July 2024.

9   TNN, 'Not Necessary That Every Ram Bhakt Will Vote for BJP: Former Madhya Pradesh CM Uma Bharti', *Times of India*, 30 June 2024, https://timesofindia.indiatimes.com/city/bhopal/not-necessary-that-every-ram-bhakt-will-vote-for-bjp-former-madhya-pradesh-cm-uma-bharti/articleshow/111374261.cms, accessed on 22 July 2024.

Chapter 4: When a Deadly Virus Meets Viral Nationalism

1   Anon, 'Prime Minister's Address to Nation Imposing 21-days Lockdown Due to COVID-19', Government of India, n.d., https://eoi.gov.in/eoisearch/MyPrint.php?10114?001/0004, accessed on 22 July 2024.

2   WION Web Team, 'India Proved Every Cynic Wrong with Its Swift Action Against COVID-19: Priyam Gandhi-Mody', WION, 21 February 2022, https://www.wionews.com/india-news/india-proved-every-cynic-wrong-with-its-swift-action-against-covid-19-priyam-gandhi-mody-455020, accessed on 22 July 2023.

3   Sharat Kumar, 'Rajasthan BJP MP Says Mud Pack, Blowing of Conch Shell Boosts Immunity Against Covid-19', *India Today*, 14 August 2020, https://www.indiatoday.in/india/story/rajasthan-bjp-mp-mud-pack-conch-shells-boost-immunity-covid-19-1710989-2020-08-14, accessed on 22 July 2024.

4   Special Correspondent, 'India Tops List of Covid-related Religious Hostilities in 2020: Pew Research Center', Telegraph Online, https://www.telegraphindia.com/india/india-tops-list-of-covid-related-religious-hostilities-in-2020-pew-research-center/cid/1901431, accessed on 22 July 2024.

5   Neetu Chandra Sharma, '30% Covid-19 Cases in India Linked to Tablighi Jamaat Event: Govt', *Mint*, 18 April 2020, https://www.livemint.com/news/india/30-covid-

19-cases-in-india-linked-to-tablighi-jamaat-event-govt-11587218560611.html, accessed on 23 July 2024.

6   Staff Reporter, 'Communalisation of COVID-19 Led to Discrimination Against Muslims', *The Hindu*, 22 January 2021, https://www.thehindu.com/news/cities/mumbai/communalisation-of-covid-19-led-to-discrimination-against-muslims/article33639018.ece, accessed on 23 July 2024.

7   Pooja Chaudhuri and Pratik Sinha, 'Video of Sufi Ritual Falsely Viral as Mass Sneezing in Nizamuddin Mosque to Spread Coronavirus Infection', Alt News, 2 April 2020, https://www.altnews.in/video-of-sufi-ritual-falsely-viral-as-mass-sneezing-in-nizamuddin-mosque-to-spread-coronavirus-infection/, accessed on 23 July 2024.

8   http://dr.ddn.upes.ac.in:8080/jspui/bitstream/123456789/2949/1/aspp.12561.pdf

9   Professor Dibyesh Anand, 'Coronavirus in India: Hindu Nationalism Being Used to Mobilise Fear During Pandemic', *News International*, 12 April 2020, https://www.thenews.com.pk/tns/detail/642322-imagining-coronajihad, accessed on 22 July 2024.

10   Mirza Ghani Baig, 'Muslim Scholars Speak Out on Tablighi Jamaat Case, Say Covid-19 Pandemic Shouldn't Be Given Communal Colour', News18, 2 April 2020, https://www.news18.com/news/india/muslim-scholars-speak-out-on-tablighi-jamaat-case-say-covid-19-pandemic-shouldnt-be-given-communal-colour-2562031.html, accessed on 22 July 2024.

11   PMO India status, https://x.com/PMOIndia/status/1251839308085915649 accessed on 1 August 2024.

12   Editorial, 'Say Sorry', *Indian Express*, 17 December 2020, https://indianexpress.com/article/opinion/editorials/tablighi-jamaat-covid-19-coronavirus-delhi-police-7107751/, accessed on 22 July 2024.

13 Nitish Kashyap, 'Bombay HC Says Tablighi Jamaat Foreigners Were Made "Scapegoats"; Quashes FIRs against Them; Criticizes Media Propaganda', *Live Law*, 22 August 2020, https://www.livelaw.in/news-updates/bombay-hc-says-tablighi-jamaat-foreigners-were-made-scapegoats-quashes-firs-against-them-criticizes-media-propaganda-161793, accessed on 22 July 2024.

Chapter 5: Nationalism Goes Global

1 Livemint, 'PM Modi Tops List of Most Popular Global Leaders with 76% Rating | Check Who's Least Popular', *Mint*, 9 December 2023, https://www.livemint.com/news/india/pm-modi-tops-list-of-most-popular-global-leaders-with-over-75-rating-check-whos-least-popular-11702050909078.html, accessed on 22 July 2024.

2 NBC News, 'What's Fueling the Rise in Hindu Nationalism in the U.S.', NBC, 27 June 2023, https://www.nbcnews.com/news/asian-america/modis-popularity-grows-india-hindu-nationalism-rising-us-rcna90680, accessed on 22 July 2024.

3 Shubhajit Roy, 'Asked about Discrimination and Dissent, Modi: Democracy in DNA', *Indian Express*, 23 June 2023, https://indianexpress.com/article/india/asked-about-discrimination-and-dissent-modi-democracy-in-dna-8680984/, accessed on 22 July 2024.

4 Soutik Biswas, '"Electoral Autocracy": The Downgrading of India's Democracy', BBC, 16 March 2021, https://www.bbc.com/news/world-asia-india-56393944, accessed on 22 July 2024.

5 PTI, 'Rahul Gandhi Arrives in San Francisco for US Visit', *Economic Times*, 30 May 2023, https://economictimes.indiatimes.com/news/politics-and-nation/rahul-gandhi-

arrives-in-san-francisco-for-us-visit/articleshow/100629453. cms?from=mdr, accessed on 22 July 2024.

6   Harish Nambiar, 'How the Great Upstart, AAP, and the Foreign Hands of Diaspora Are Changing Politics in Punjab', *Economic Times*, 5 February 2017, https://economictimes. indiatimes.com/news/politics-and-nation/how-the-great-upstart-aap-and-the-foreign-hands-of-diaspora-are-changing-politics-in-punjab/articleshow/56975837. cms?from=mdr, accessed on 22 July 2024.

Chapter 6: Political Tricolour and Soft Hindutva

1   Shaju Philip and Manoj G.C., 'Antony Touches Raw "Secular" Nerve, Says Cong's "Proximity to Minority Communities" Leads to "Doubt"', *Indian Express*, 28 June 2014, https://indianexpress.com/article/political-pulse/ antony-touches-raw-secular-nerve/, accessed on 22 July 2024.

2   Yogendra Yadav, 'The 4 Cs That Mark Congress' Decline from Secularism to Soft Hindutva', Print, 3 January 2024, https://theprint.in/opinion/the-4-cs-that-mark-congress-decline-from-secularism-to-soft-hindutva/152556/, accessed on 22 July 2024.

3   Vinayak Damodar Savarkar was a Hindu nationalist and leading figure in the Hindu Mahasabha, a Hindu nationalist organization and political party. His definition of Hindutva is seen as a precursor to the modern Hindu nationalist movement.

4   PTI, 'Two Years Ago, Still Relevant: Shashi Tharoor on Old Post Comparing Hinduism, Hindutva', *Times of India*, 29 December 2021, https://timesofindia. indiatimes.com/india/two-years-ago-still-relevant-shashi-tharoor-on-old-post-comparing-hinduism-hindutva/ articleshow/88557061.cms., accessed on 22 July 2024.

5   Rahul Gandhi, 'Rahul Gandhi Writes: Satyam Shivam Sundaram', *Indian Express*, 3 October 2024, https://indianexpress.com/article/opinion/columns/rahul-gandhi-opinion-on-hinduism-8963249/, accessed on 22 July 2024.

Chapter 7: Reimagining the Poll Plan

1   PTI and Business Standard, 'Time to Hail India–UAE Partnership: PM Modi at Diaspora Event in Abu Dhabi', *Business Standard*, 13 February 2024, https://www.business-standard.com/world-news/time-to-hail-india-uae-partnership-pm-modi-at-diaspora-event-in-abu-dhabi-124021301622_1.html, accessed on 22 July 2024.
2   ANI, 'Modi Reaches Out to Minorities', Business Standard Online, 25 May 2019, https://www.business-standard.com/article/news-ani/modi-reaches-out-to-minorities-119052500924_1.html, accessed on 22 July 2024.
3   INC India, https://x.com/INCIndia/status/1533716570773590016?lang=en
4   Special Correspondent, 'PM, Home Minister and RSS Responsible for Creating Atmosphere of Hatred: Rahul Gandhi', *The Hindu*, 1 July 2022, https://www.thehindu.com/news/national/pm-home-minister-and-rss-responsible-for-creating-atmosphere-of-hatred-rahul-gandhi/article65590018.ece, accessed on 22 July 2024.

Chapter 8: Of Ideology and Semantics; New Parliament and New Names

1   Anon, 'PM's Address at the Celebration of Dedication of New Parliament Building to the Nation', n.d., https://www.pmindia.gov.in/en/news_updates/pms-address-at-the-

celebration-of-dedication-of-new-parliament-building-to-the-nation/, accessed on 22 July 2024.

2   The Hindu Bureau, 'Opposition Dubs New Parliament Inauguration "Self-glorification and Coronation"', *The Hindu*, 28 May 2023, https://www.thehindu.com/news/national/likening-it-to-a-coronation-opposition-boycotts-parliament-inauguration/article66905031.ece., accessed on 22 July 2024.

3   The Hindu Bureau, '19 Opposition Parties, Including Congress, to Boycott Inauguration of New Parliament Building', *The Hindu*, 28 September 2023, https://www.thehindu.com/news/national/19-opposition-parties-including-congress-to-boycott-inauguration-of-new-parliament-building/article66887824.ece#:~:text=Their%20primary%20objection%20is%20against,which%20demands%20a%20commensurate%20response%E2%80%9D., accessed on 22 July 2024.

4   Damini Nath, 'All Parties Invited . . . Don't Link It to Politics: Shah', *Indian Express*, 25 May 2023, https://indianexpress.com/article/india/pm-modi-bjp-govt-report-card-parliament-building-amit-shah-8625997/, accessed on 22 July 2024.

5   ETV Bharat, 'PM Modi Will Receive "Sengol" from Tamil Nadu Saivite Mutt Adheenam, Install in New Parliament: Amit Shah', ETV Bharat News, 24 May 2023, https://www.etvbharat.com/english/state/delhi/union-minister-amit-shah-on-new-parliament/na20230524123505457457106., accessed on 22 July 2024.

6   Rajeev Dikshit, 'India Rebuilding Symbols of Its Faith & Culture: PM Modi', *Times of India*, 18 December 2023, https://timesofindia.indiatimes.com/india/india-rebuilding-symbols-of-its-faith-culture-pm-modi/articleshow/106105109.cms, accessed on 22 July 2024.

7   Bikash Singh, 'Do Not Use India, Instead Use the Word Bharat: RSS Chief Mohan Bhagwat', *Economic Times*, 3 September 2023, https://economictimes.indiatimes. com/news/politics-and-nation/do-not-use-india-instead-use-the-word-bharat-rss-chief-mohan-bhagwat/ articleshow/103291950.cms?from=mdr., accessed on 22 July 2024.

8   Virender Sehwag, https://x.com/virendersehwag/status/ 1698974153389531617?lang=en

9   ANI, 'No One Can Stop Us from Rewriting Our History: Union Home Minister Amit Shah', *Economic Times*, 25 November 2022, https://economictimes.indiatimes.com/ news/politics-and-nation/no-one-can-stop-us-from-rewriting-our-history-union-home-minister-amit-shah/articleshow/95761103.cms?from=mdr., accessed on 22 July 2024.

10   https://www.thehindu.com/news/national/historians-condemn-key-deletions-from-ncert-textbooks/ article66711848.ece

11   The Hindu Bureau, 'Historians Condemn Key Deletions from NCERT Textbooks', *The Hindu*, 8 April 2023, https:// www.thehindu.com/news/national/historians-condemn-key-deletions-from-ncert-textbooks/article66711848.ece., accessed on 22 July 2024.

12   Manu S Pillai, 'If Mughals Were Violent, so Were Hindu Kings', *Times of India*, 13 April 2023, https:// timesofindia.indiatimes.com/india/really-royally-bloody/ articleshow/99471383.cms, accessed on 22 July 2024.

13   DC Correspondent, 'PM Modi's Gift to Biden for Seeing 1,000 Full Moons in his Life', *Deccan Chronicle*, 22 June 2023, https://www.deccanchronicle.com/nation/in-other-news/220623/sandalwood-box-green-diamond-pm-

modis-unique-gifts-to-joe-biden-fi.html, accessed on 22 July 2024.

14 Express Web Desk, 'Taj Mahal Doesn't Reflect Indian Culture: Yogi Adityanath', *Indian Express*, 16 June 2017, https://indianexpress.com/article/india/yogi-adityanath-narendra-modi-achievements-gifted-with-gita-taj-mahal-replica-foreign-dignitaries-4707585/, accessed on 22 July 2024.

Chapter 9: Popular Culture: The New Battleground

1 Himanshu Mishra, 'PM Modi Tells BJP MPs *The Kashmir Files* Is a Good Film, Everyone Should Watch It', *India Today*, 15 March 2022, https://www.indiatoday.in/india/story/pm-modi-kashmir-files-good-film-everyone-should-watch-bjp-meet-1925518-2022-03-15#:~:text=Prime%20Minister%20Narendra%20Modi%20asked,of%20you%20should%20watch%20it, accessed on 22 July 2024.

2 PTI, '*The Kerala Story* Is RSS Agenda to Humiliate the State, Says CM Pinarayi Vijayan', 9 April 2024, https://indianexpress.com/article/india/pinarayi-vijayan-kerala-story-film-rss-agenda-9259887/, accessed on 22 July 2024.

3 Amit Malviya, https://x.com/amitmalviya/status/1651193185979490306?lang=en

4 Paran Balakrishnan, 'Box-Office Success of *Kashmir Files*, *Kerala Story* Fuels More Propagandist Cinema', *Telegraph*, 22 June 2023, https://www.telegraphindia.com/india/box-office-success-of-kashmir-files-kerala-story-fuels-more-propagandist-cinema/cid/1946947#:~:text=But%20I%20knew%20The%20

Kashmir,been%20taking%20over%20our%20screens, accessed on 22 July 2023.

5   Shreevatsa Nevatia, 'Intolerance and Outrage Leave Indian Stand-up Comics with Less to Laugh About', *Frontline*, 28 November 2023, https://frontline.thehindu.com/society/intolerance-outrage-leaving-indian-stand-up-comics-with-less-to-laugh-about/article67511887.ece., accessed on 22 July 2024.

6   Hindustantimes.com, 'Who Is Munawar Faruqui? Why Was He Arrested?', *Hindustan Times*, 5 February 2021, https://www.hindustantimes.com/india-news/who-is-munawar-faruqui-why-was-he-arrested-101612515403257.html.

7   Sonam Saigal, 'Vir Das | The Comedian from Two Indias', *The Hindu*, 21 November 2021, https://www.thehindu.com/news/national/vir-das-the-comedian-from-two-indias/article37600621.ece., accessed on 22 July 2024.

8   BBC News, 'Comedian Vir Das Causes a Stir with "Two Indias" Monologue', BBC, 17 November 2021, https://www.bbc.com/news/world-asia-india-59323282., accessed on 22 July 2024.

9   PTI, 'Comic Vir Das Clarifies on Viral "I Come from 2 Indias" Monologue', NDTV, 17 November 2021, https://www.ndtv.com/india-news/dont-be-fooled-vir-das-clarifies-i-come-from-2-indias-monologue-2613796, accessed on 22 July 2024.

10   Neeti Palta, 'India's Standup Comics Need Quick Wit, Quicker Legs and Lawyer on Speed Dial', Print, 7 January 2021, https://theprint.in/opinion/indias-standup-comics-need-quick-wit-quicker-legs-and-lawyer-on-speed-dial-neeti-palta/580826/., accessed on 22 July 2024.

Chapter 10: Boycott Culture: The Beginning of the End?

1   Sushmita Dey, 'Filmmaker Madhur Bhandarkar REACTS to Boycott Bollywood Trend: It Happened after Sushant Singh Rajput's Death', *Times Now*, 10 May 2023, https://www.timesnownews.com/entertainment-news/filmmaker-madhur-bhandarkar-reacts-to-boycott-bollywood-trend-it-happened-after-sushant-singh-rajputs-death-bollywood-news-article-100119613#:~:text=During%20a%20conversation%20with%20Maniesh,Maybe%20the%20industry%20ignored%20him%E2%80%A6., accessed on 22 July 2024.

2   Taran Adarsh, 'STOP Being in Denial about #Boycott Calls *Not* Affecting Film Biz . . . The Fact Is, These #Boycott Calls *HAVE* Made a . . .', LinkedIn, 13 August 2022, https://www.linkedin.com/posts/taran-adarsh-07a280178_boycott-boycott-bo-activity-6964224012222672896-_hcI?trk=public_profile_like_view., accessed on 22 July 2024.

3   Himanshu Mishra, 'Refrain from Unnecessary Remarks on Films: PM Modi's Diktat to BJP Leaders', *India Today*, 17 January 2023, https://www.indiatoday.in/india/story/refrain-from-making-unnecessary-remarks-on-films-pm-modis-diktat-to-bjp-leaders-2322830-2023-01-17., accessed on 22 July 2024.

4   Hannah Ellis-Petersen, 'Pathaan and the King of Cinema Blast Bollywood Out of the Doldrums', *Guardian*, 4 February 2023, https://www.theguardian.com/film/2023/feb/04/pathaan-shah-rukh-khan-bollywood-out-of-doldrums., accessed on 22 July 2024.

5   Anon, 'Recovery in Youth Employment Is Still Lagging, Says ILO,' International Labour Organization, 1 February

2024, https://www.ilo.org/resource/news/recovery-youth-employment-still-lagging-says-ilo-0#:~:text=The%20 total%20global%20number%20of,of%202019%2C%20 the%20report%20says, accessed on 22 July 2024.

6   Outlook Web Desk, 'OTT Platforms under Pressure to Censor Projects Involving Political, Religious Sentiments: Report', *Outlook India*, 18 January 2024, https://www.outlookindia. com/culture-society/ott-platforms-netflix-amazon-prime-video-under-pressure-to-censor-projects-involving-political-religious-sentiments-report-news-332202#:~:text=In-dian%20filmmaker%20Anurag%20Kashyap%2C%20 who,Maximum%20City%E2%80%9D%2C%20which%20 explores%20the., accessed on 22 July 2024.

Chapter 11: The Legend of Ram

1   Anon., 'English Rendering of PM's Address at the Pran-Pratishtha of Shree Ram Lalla at Ayodhya Ji', PIB, 22 January 2024, https://pib.gov.in/PressReleasePage. aspx?PRID=1998560, accessed on 22 July 2024.

2   ET Online, 'Pran-Pratishtha Ceremony: Taiwan's Foreign Minister Conveys Deep Sentiments on Ram Mandir', *Economic Times*, 23 January 2024, https://economictimes. indiatimes.com/news/india/pran-pratishtha-ceremony-taiwans-foreign-minister-conveys-deep-sentiments-on-ram-mandir/videoshow/107088184.cms?from=mdr, accessed on 22 July 2024.

3   Ronit Singh, 'Ram Mandir LIVE: Ayodhya's Ram Temple Lit up Ahead of Pran Pratistha Ceremony', Republic World, 21 January 2024, https://www.republicworld.com/ india/ram-mandir-live-pran-pratishtha-january-21-latest-updates-ayodhya-ram-janmabhoomi-temple, accessed on 22 July 2024.

4   ET Online, 'The Temple of Development: How Ayodhya Will Prove to Be an Economic Boost', *Economic Times*, 22 January 2024, https://economictimes.indiatimes.com/news/india/the-temple-of-development-how-ayodhya-will-prove-to-be-an-economic-boost/articleshow/106580290.cms?from=mdr, accessed on 22 July 2024.

5   Ashutosh Kumar, 'Ram Mandir Fillip to Fetch Revenues Worth Rs 2500 Crore to UP in FY25: SBI', *Fortune India*, 22 January 2024, https://www.fortuneindia.com/macro/ram-mandir-fillip-to-fetch-revenues-worth-25000-crore-to-up-in-fy25-sbi/115478#:~:text="Given%20the%20completion%20of%20Ram,earn%20an%20additional%20tax%20revenue

6   Admin, 'PM inaugurates, dedicates to nation and lays the foundation stone of multiple development projects worth more than Rs 15,700 crore', Narendra Modi, 30 December 2023, https://www.narendramodi.in/prime-minister-narendra-modi-lays-foundation-and-inuagurates-various-projects-in-ayodhya-577602, accessed on 22 July 2024.

7   ET Online, 'The Temple of Development: How Ayodhya Will Prove to Be an Economic Boost', *Economic Times*, 22 January 2024, https://economictimes.indiatimes.com/news/india/the-temple-of-development-how-ayodhya-will-prove-to-be-an-economic-boost/articleshow/106580290.cms?from=mdr#:~:text=Rs%2085%2C000%20crore%20makeover,this%20month%2C%20TOI%20has%20' accessed on 22 July 2024.

8   https://www.youtube.com/watch?v=3A8BmbXT6Gw&feature=youtu.be.

9   Abhishek De, 'In PM Modi's Temple Visits, a Ramayana Trail Emerges', *India Today*, 22 January 2024, https://www.indiatoday.in/india/story/ram-mandir-ayodhya-pran-pratishtha-pm-modi-temple-visits-ramayana-lord-ram-route-2491050-2024-01-20, accessed on 22 January 2024.

Acknowledgements

Narendra Nath Mishra

Writing a book? It's like a creative pregnancy for any author, filled with many challenges, much pain, the eagerness hidden behind that pain and the impatience for that special day. Clearly, this journey was filled with all shades of experiences and emotions. And today, as the book has reached its destination, it is essential to express gratitude to the witnesses and supporters of this journey. Because they were with us, we reached this point, with the book among you. First and foremost, thanks to my co-author Marya Shakil. Can you believe that we wrote it smoothly without any conflicts? While you will have to read the book to assess Marya's authorship, I can attest she an exceptional human being.

Then, thanks to the publisher Milee, who became our Barack Obama. Successfully explained—yes we can. And we proved it. Thanks for boosting our courage and giving us the opportunity.

Then all the colleagues, friends and all those people with their input, with whom we conversed and whose boundless knowledge developed our understanding. They helped in presenting it in a better way.

Finally, you cannot forget to express gratitude to your family who remained the biggest support throughout the entire process. Like father, Rama Nath Mishra, who always stood behind me like a pillar, ensuring that son Tuhin manages his studies and other things better so that a father's stress is not there. And last but not the least, my wife, Rama, without whom every word would remain incomplete.

Marya Shakil

I would like to begin by thanking my co-author and fellow Bihari, Narendra, for being my friend, philosopher and guide through and through. His world view often helps in bringing the best out of me. Milee, my classmate from Patna, who, for years, had been persuading me to write a book. Thank you for making this entire exercise so smooth and navigating with us through tight deadlines while understanding our professional compulsions. My papa, late Shakil Ahmad Khan, was my biggest cheerleader as I put together this book. I would like to remember him for instilling in me diligence and resilience. My husband, Irfan, who epitomises patience, love and support. A word for my ammi for her constant dua and faith. My sisters, Apa and Fauzia, for taking up the good fight and being my conscience keeper. Thank you, Abbu, my father-in-law for asking me every time he saw me about the status of my book.

Scan QR code to access the
Penguin Random House India website